Ethics and the Law on End-of-Life Decisions in Malaysia

Fadhlina Alias • Puteri Nemie Jahn Kassim

Ethics and the Law on End-of-Life Decisions in Malaysia

Springer

Fadhlina Alias
Faculty of Syariah and Law
Universiti Sains Islam Malaysia
Nilai, Negeri Sembilan, Malaysia

Puteri Nemie Jahn Kassim
Ahmad Ibrahim Kulliyyah of Laws
International Islamic University Malaysia
Kuala Lumpur, Malaysia

ISBN 978-981-92-3624-4 ISBN 978-981-92-3625-1 (eBook)
https://doi.org/10.1007/978-981-92-3625-1

This Springer imprint is published by the registered company Springer Nature Singapore Pte Ltd.
The registered company address is: 152 Beach Road, #21-01/04 Gateway East, Singapore 189721, Singapore

To my most beloved late parents, Dr. Rohani Ahmad and Dr. Alias Kamis, whose unconditional love and unwavering faith in me continue to be a beacon throughout my life journey. Through them, I have come to understand the true meaning of the words of Prophet Muhammad (peace and blessings be upon him):
"The best of people are those who are most beneficial to others".
Until we meet again
in the gardens of eternal peace,
where hearts are at ease
and only blessings remain.

Foreword

It is my honour and privilege to be invited to pen the foreword for this book on *Ethics and the Law on End-of-Life Decisions in Malaysia*.

Advancements in medicine have successfully extended our life expectancy rates and significantly reduced illness-related morbidity. Nevertheless, the elixir of immortality has remained elusive. The Latin phrase *memento mori* reminds us of our mortality and the inevitability of death. While many may not be comfortable to initiate or be involved in a discussion on this topic, as living beings, each one of us will need to embrace death as a certainty.

In the clinical setting, end-of-life practices continue to evolve based not only on scientific evidence, but also on socio-religious-cultural factors. However, advancements in this field do not necessarily just mean "more treatment". It is also addressed by how we can afford patients "more comfort", "more dignity" and "more meaning" to their suffering. Decisions that are made about our end-of-life choices often highlight the complexities in the perennial debate about weighing the quantity of life versus the quality of life, and the position of the sanctity of life. As humans, we are social beings, and the rationale for these decisions that are made at such a critical point in our lives often uncovers philosophical roots that are manifested and result in practical realities that not only affect us individually, but also bear an impact on those who surround us—our families, friends, community and society.

In this book, readers are brought by the authors on a journey to unravel the complexities that surround end-of-life decision-making in Malaysia. It begins with a description of the conceptual and contextual foundations of end-of-life decisions in Malaysia. The authors then consider the ethical dimensions and legal issues related to end-of-life decision-making before shifting the focus to an examination of the current regulatory frameworks on end-of-life decisions in Malaysia. Following this, they then set the foundation for moving towards a coherent ethico-legal framework that is so needed in Malaysia before providing tangible proposals for how the future direction for holistic regulatory reforms in this area should entail. These include the avoidance of misleading terminology such as "passive euthanasia", clearer legal protection for doctors, the promotion of advance decision-making tools such as advance care planning, the need for mental capacity legislation, and the importance of cultural competence as well as profession and ethical conduct.

The discussions, debates and analysis in this book are timely for two reasons. Firstly, the World Bank projects that Malaysia will move from being an upper-middle income developing country into a high-income developed country between 2028 and 2030. Secondly, Malaysia is currently an ageing society and is projected to transition into an "aged nation" by 2045. As we stand at the threshold of these two significant transitions, issues surrounding end-of-life decisions need to be examined and contextualised to our local setting. This decolonising process requires careful consideration of the societal values and cultural norms to develop suitable and meaningful ethico-legal frameworks that guide the development of medical practice in this area in Malaysia.

As a clinical ethicist, I am able to attest to the fact that some of the most complex and diverse ethical dilemmas related to medicine are often found in end-of-life decision-making. In manoeuvring through them, I am often reminded of this quote by Edmund Pellegrino, a key pioneer in clinical bioethics and the philosophy of medicine, who said that medicine is "the most humane of sciences, the most empiric of arts, and the most scientific of humanities". As we engage with the contents of this book, and the dilemmas and debates on end-of-life decisions in Malaysia, I urge you to consider how we are able to reconcile the science of medical advancements at the end of life with the art of dying well.

It is my hope that this book will prove to be a seminal text on end-of-life decision-making in Malaysia, and I am sure that will not only benefit scholars of medical law and bioethics, medical and legal practitioners, policymakers and students, but everyone who engages with its content—for all of us will be called upon to make such decisions at some points in our lives—be it for ourselves or for others.

Lastly, allow me to conclude with one last consideration on this topic, which is illustrated with a quote from Dame Cicely Saunders who pioneered the modern hospice movement, that "how people die remains in the memory of those who live on". Congratulations to the authors on the production of this scholarly work, and may it enhance our understanding, create even more awareness, and guide us in making good decisions about the end of life.

Monash University Malaysia, Bandar Sunway, Malaysia
Member, National Bioethics Council, Wilayah Persekutuan Putrajaya, Malaysia

23 May 2026 Mark Kiak Min Tan

Preface

End-of-life care is an area of medical practice where questions of law, ethics, religion, culture and clinical judgement often meet in difficult and sensitive circumstances. Advances in modern medicine have made it possible to prolong life in ways that were once not medically possible. While this has brought considerable benefit to patients and families, it has also raised difficult questions on when treatment should be continued, withheld or withdrawn, how suffering should be relieved, and how decisions ought to be made when a patient is approaching the end of life.

These questions are especially important because they are rarely abstract. They arise at moments of vulnerability, when patients may be seriously ill, families may be emotionally distressed, and doctors may be required to make decisions under considerable professional and moral pressure. In such circumstances, the absence of clear legal standards may create uncertainty for all parties involved. It may leave doctors unsure of the extent of their legal protection, patients uncertain as to whether their wishes will be respected, and families without sufficient guidance in making or participating in difficult decisions.

This book is written against that background. Its central concern is the need for a coherent ethico-legal framework on end-of-life decisions in Malaysia. Existing ethical codes, professional guidelines, palliative care standards and recent developments on advance care planning and consent have contributed meaningfully to the development of medical practice in this area. Nevertheless, important issues are yet to be addressed with sufficient legal clarity, particularly in relation to withholding and withdrawal of life-sustaining treatment, palliative measures that may foreseeably hasten death, advance decisions, surrogate decision-making, mental capacity and the legal protection of doctors who act in good faith and in accordance with proper professional standards.

The need for clearer guidance must also be understood within Malaysia's own social and normative setting. End-of-life decisions in Malaysia cannot be separated from religious belief, cultural values, family involvement and the realities of medical practice. For that reason, any proposed framework should not proceed on the basis of adopting foreign models without due regard to local circumstances. While the common law experience of jurisdictions such as the United Kingdom and

Australia offers useful points of reference, the development of Malaysian standards must remain attentive to local legal, professional and social circumstances.

At the same time, sensitivity to local context should not result in the continued absence of clear standards. End-of-life decisions concern matters of profound importance: the dignity of the patient, the relief of suffering, the role of the family, the professional duties of doctors and the limits of medical intervention. A more coherent framework would not remove the emotional difficulty of such decisions, but it may provide a firmer basis upon which they can be made with greater clarity, legitimacy and compassion.

This book therefore seeks to examine end-of-life decisions in Malaysia through an integrated ethico-legal lens. It considers the ethical principles that inform medical decision-making, including the manner in which these principles are reflected in Malaysian professional ethical guidance. It then examines common law principles developed in comparable jurisdictions, not as models to be adopted without qualification, but as sources of reasoning that may assist in addressing areas where Malaysian law remains unclear. The discussion thereafter turns to the adequacy of the current Malaysian statutory and regulatory position. Its purpose is not to reduce end-of-life care to a question of legal compliance, but to consider how law may better support ethical, compassionate and professionally responsible medical practice.

The book is intended for legal scholars, medical law and bioethics researchers, healthcare professionals, policymakers, postgraduate students and readers with an interest in the development of palliative and end-of-life care in Malaysia. It is hoped that the discussion will contribute to a more coherent and locally responsive understanding of how patients, families and doctors may be better supported in navigating decisions at the end of life.

Nilai, Malaysia — Fadhlina Alias
Kuala Lumpur, Malaysia — Puteri Nemie Jahn Kassim

Acknowledgements All Praise to Allah, the Bestower of Faith, the Most Compassionate and the Most Beneficent, for it is only by His Will and His Guidance that this book has been made possible.

This work would not have come to completion without the support, guidance and kindness of many individuals and institutions. We wish to express our deepest appreciation to the Springer editorial team, especially our editor, Alexandra Campbell, whose counsel, patience, encouragement and invaluable support have accompanied us throughout the publication process. We are truly grateful for her confidence in this project and for the care with which she has guided it from its early stages to completion.

We would also like to convey our sincere gratitude to the reviewers of this book for their thoughtful reading, valuable insights and constructive feedback. Their comments have helped us reflect more carefully on our arguments and have contributed meaningfully to the refinement of this book.

A special note of appreciation is extended to Dr. Mark Tan for graciously writing the foreword to this book. His willingness to lend his voice to this work is indeed an honour, particularly given his long-standing engagement with the field and his familiarity with our work.

Profound thanks are also due to our colleagues, whose words of encouragement and goodwill have meant a great deal to us throughout the writing process. We are equally grateful to our respective institutions, Universiti Sains Islam Malaysia and International Islamic University Malaysia, for providing the institutional and academic support that enabled us to undertake and complete this project.

This book has been shaped by an academic relationship that we both value deeply. What began as a supervisor–student relationship has grown into a collegial and scholarly collaboration founded on mutual respect, trust and intellectual openness. Over time, the mentoring relationship between teacher and student has also grown into a close friendship, held with gratitude and affection. We are grateful for the opportunity to have brought this work to completion together, and for the many conversations, reflections and shared commitments that have enriched the process.

Although this book is a collaboration, we wish to record our personal appreciation to those closest to us, whose devotion and quiet sacrifices have carried us through this undertaking.

Fadhlina would like to express her heartfelt gratitude to her husband, Mohd Fairuz, her only sibling, Ahmad Fadhil and his wife, Helwa Husna, as well as her other family members and relatives, for their patience, prayers, advice, understanding and unwavering support throughout the writing process. Their love, encouragement and faith have been a constant source of strength, especially during the most demanding moments of this journey.

Puteri Nemie wishes to express her deepest appreciation to her beloved family, whose love, prayers and quiet encouragement have accompanied her throughout the preparation of this book. Their understanding and steadfast support have brought comfort and remained an important source of reassurance throughout this endeavour.

Finally, we wish to thank everyone who has contributed to this book, whether through intellectual guidance, professional support, personal encouragement or prayers. This work has come to fruition not only through our own efforts, but also through the generosity, kindness and support of many others. Any errors or omissions that remain are, of course, entirely our own.

Competing Interests The authors have no competing interests to declare that are relevant to the content of this manuscript.

Contents

About the Authors

Fadhlina Alias is an Associate Professor at the Faculty of Syariah and Law, Universiti Sains Islam Malaysia. She holds an LLB (Hons) and a Doctor of Philosophy in Law from the International Islamic University Malaysia (IIUM), as well as an LLM in International Commercial Law from the University of Nottingham, United Kingdom. Her primary research interests are in medical law and bioethics, with a sustained focus on the ethico-legal aspects of end-of-life care in Malaysia. She is the author of *Medical Decisions at the End of Life: An Islamic Perspective* and has actively published in the areas of patient autonomy, medical decision-making and the regulation of end-of-life decisions. Her scholarship engages with the intersection of law, medicine and Islamic ethics, and contributes to the growing body of Malaysian literature on medical law reform, professional guidance and the ethical management of end-of-life care.

Puteri Nemie Jahn Kassim is a Professor at the Civil Law Department, Ahmad Ibrahim Kulliyyah of Laws, IIUM. She obtained her LLB (Hons) degree from the University of Southampton, United Kingdom and completed her postgraduate studies (Master of Comparative Laws and Doctor of Philosophy in Law) at IIUM. She currently teaches Law of Torts and Medical Law at the undergraduate level and Medical Negligence Law at the postgraduate level. Her other published books include *Nursing Law and Ethics*, *Medical Negligence Law in Malaysia*, *Law and Ethics Relating to the Medical Profession* and *Medical Negligence in Malaysia: Cases and Commentary*. Puteri Nemie is a prolific writer of articles and a regular presenter at seminars and conferences both locally and at the international level.

Chapter 1
Conceptual and Contextual Foundations of End-of-Life Decisions in Malaysia

Abstract This chapter lays the foundation for the discussion on end-of-life decisions in Malaysia by establishing the conceptual, social and legal foundations within which such decisions arise. It begins by examining the meaning and scope of end-of-life care and clarifying its relationship with supportive care, palliative care and hospice care. The chapter then identifies the principal medical decisions that arise at the end of life, including active euthanasia, assisted dying or assisted suicide, withholding and withdrawal of treatment and pain management in the form of palliative and terminal sedation. It further traces the development of palliative care in Malaysia, drawing attention to recent policy and service developments as well as the continuing challenges relating to access, integration and quality of care. The discussion also situates end-of-life care within Malaysia's socioreligious context, highlighting the significance of religion, spirituality and family-centred decision-making in a plural society. In this light, the chapter considers religious guidance on end-of-life decisions, with emphasis on the Islamic perspective alongside the broader multi-faith landscape in Malaysia. It concludes by explaining the relevance of common law in the Malaysian legal system and its continuing importance in shaping the medicolegal analysis of end-of-life decisions.

1.1 Introduction

Death and dying are, more often than not, highly charged topics due to the sense of loss, fear and uncertainty that one experiences at the end of life. In modern times, this is further augmented by the presence of medical interventions that are able to prolong the life expectancy of the critically ill, which has redefined the once clear demarcation between life and death. In a healthcare setting, decisions made during the patient's terminal stage involve considerations that extend beyond the physical care of the patient, and because the dying process has a profound effect not only on the patient but also on family members, their wishes form an indispensable component in the decision-making process. Thus, the care system at the end of life does not only consist of doctors but a team of professionals from various disciplines of

F. Alias, P. N. Jahn Kassim, *Ethics and the Law on End-of-Life Decisions in Malaysia*, https://doi.org/10.1007/978-981-92-3625-1_1

both social and healthcare to ensure that the patient's comfort and needs are attended to.

In discussing the process of care when a patient approaches and enters the dying stage, it is important to understand what it entails, including the terms, concepts, scope and medical actions that are associated with it. This also necessitates a deliberation on the issue of euthanasia, which is ineludibly pertinent when the process of dying in a clinical setting is broached. At the same time, end-of-life care cannot be examined in isolation from the broader setting in which it is practised. In Malaysia, this includes the development of palliative care services, the socioreligious realities of a multi-faith society, the significance of religious guidance in shaping attitudes towards death and dying and the relevance of common law principles in addressing questions for which local legislation remains limited. This chapter therefore introduces the conceptual framework of end-of-life care, the scope of the principal decisions that arise at this stage and the broader Malaysian context within which the ensuing ethical, religious and legal discussions in this book are situated.

1.2 Conceptual Framework of End-of-Life Care

The term "end-of-life care" is generally used to refer to the health and social care system required to address the physical, spiritual, emotional and social needs of patients who are suffering from serious illnesses or incurable diseases or are in the final stages of their lives and includes acute care and long-term care. From the healthcare perspective, end-of-life care encompasses multiple forms of care such as supportive care, palliative care and hospice care and focuses more on providing a comfortable environment to restore and improve patients' quality of life as far as it is practically possible.

The use of the term "end-of-life care" in relation to palliative care however has been met with criticism by some experts directly involved in the field of palliative medicine. Tallon argues that it is not easy to define "end-of-life care"; on the one hand, it is considered synonymous with palliative care, which aims to provide comfort and quality of life as best as possible for terminally ill patients, yet at the same time, the term is identifiable as only a small segment of palliative care that focuses on the dying process which may be difficult to ascertain.[1] Palliative specialists such as Davis and Kuebler, however, aver that the connotation in which "end-of-life care" is commonly used is in fact misleading and should not be used interchangeably with palliative care or hospice care.[2] They contend that while hospice care and end-of-life care are both components of palliative care and/or supportive care, the reverse is not always true. The primary concern raised is that "end-of-life care" is a quantitative term denoting time-defined care that excludes the purpose of care and

[1] Tallon (2012), p. 2.

[2] Davis and Kuebler (2007), p. 24.

fails to recognise the complex sets of skills inherent in good palliative medicine. This is as opposed to palliative care which is goal-oriented and is not confined to terminally ill patients or those at the end of life.

In order to facilitate better understanding of the factual context of the different terms used in correlation with end-of-life care, it is necessary to define what is meant by "supportive care", "palliative care" and "hospice care".

1.2.1 Supportive Care

There appears to be a lack of a standardised definition of "supportive care" in medical literature. The working definition suggested by the National Council for Hospice and Specialist Palliative Care Services in the UK is that supportive care is a form of framework that "helps the patient and their family to cope with cancer and treatment of it—from pre-diagnosis, through the process of diagnosis and treatment, to cure, continuing illness or death and into bereavement. It helps the patient to maximise the benefits of treatment and to live as well as possible with the effects of the disease. It is given equal priority alongside diagnosis and treatment."[3] According to the Multinational Association of Supportive Care in Cancer, the term "supportive care" refers to "the prevention and management of the adverse effects of cancer and its treatment. This includes management of physical and psychological symptoms and side effects across the continuum of the cancer experience from diagnosis through anticancer treatment to post-treatment care. Enhancing rehabilitation, secondary cancer prevention, survivorship and end of life care are integral to supportive care".[4] The European Society of Medical Oncology (ESMO) adopts the following definition: Supportive care is that which "aims to optimise the comfort, function and social support of the patients and their family at all stages of the illness. This dimension of care emphasises the oncologist's role in optimizing quality of life for all patients, including those with potentially curative illness".[5] A broader description of the term is offered by Berger, Portenoy and Weissman, in that it covers aspects of medical care which are concerned with the physical, psychosocial and spiritual issues faced by cancer patients and their respective families, communities and health providers.[6] In this context, supportive oncology refers to both interventions used to support patients who experience adverse effects caused by antineoplastic

---

[3] National Institute for Clinical Excellence (2004), p. 18. The National Institute for Clinical Excellence Guidance sets out the scope of supportive care to encompass (1) self-help and support, (2) participation of patient and caretakers in the development of services, (3) proper and effective dissemination of information, (4) psychological support, (5) symptom control, (6) social support, (7) rehabilitation, (8) complementary therapies, (9) spiritual support, (10) palliative care and (11) end-of-life and bereavement care.

[4] Multinational Association of Supportive Care in Cancer (2013).

[5] See Cherny (2003), pp. 1335–1337.

[6] See Berger et al. (1998).

therapies and those interventions which are considered to be under the broad spectrum of palliative care.

Hui suggests that a proper conceptual framework with regard to supportive care is best reflected in the following definition: "...the provision of the necessary services for those living with or affected by cancer to meet their informational, emotional, spiritual, social, or physical needs during their diagnostic, treatment, or follow-up phases encompassing issues of health promotion and prevention, survivorship, palliation, and bereavement".[7] He considers this to be a broader definition that comprehensively covers the three key components: the target group, the time-frame and domains of care.

Although differences of opinion exist as to the precise connotation of "supportive care", several consistent inferences can be drawn therefrom:

(a) Supportive care involves symptom management and improvement of quality of life of patients suffering from both incurable and curable diseases.
(b) The aim of supportive care extends beyond the provision of clinical interventions or symptomatic therapy and includes psychological, social and spiritual support for the patients and their families.
(c) Supportive care is not confined to any particular phase of the illness and is provided from the pre-diagnostic stage until the end-of-life and bereavement phase.

1.2.2 Palliative Care

The word "palliate" originates from the Latin verb *palliatus* which means "to be cloaked or shielded". In the context of healthcare, the *Oxford English Dictionary* defines "palliate" as "to make (a disease or its symptoms) less severe without removing the cause". Taken literally, this appears to restrict palliative care to refer to the provision of care in the form of symptomatic relief that is not intended to be curative. The widely recognised definition of palliative care, however, is that which was drafted by the World Health Organization in 2002 (WHO). The WHO defines "palliative care" as "an approach that improves the quality of life of patients and their families facing the problem associated with life-threatening illness, through the prevention and relief of suffering by means of early identification and impeccable assessment and treatment of pain and other problems, physical, psychosocial and spiritual".[8] A corresponding description is provided by the National Institute of Clinical Excellence (NICE) in the UK: Palliative care is "the active holistic care of patients with advanced, progressive illness. Management of pain and other symptoms and provision of psychological, social and spiritual support is paramount. The goal of palliative care is achievement of the best quality of life for patients and their families. Many aspects of palliative care are also applicable earlier in the course of

[7] Hui (2014), p. 374.

[8] World Health Organization (2002), p. 84.

the illness in conjunction with other treatments".[9] Similarly, the view of the WHO is also endorsed by ESMO, which refers to palliative care as "care that that aims to optimize the comfort, function and social support of the patients and their family when cure is not possible. This dimension of care emphasizes the special needs of patients whose illness is either unlikely to be cured or that is incurable. These needs include physical and psychological symptom control, education and optimization of community supports".[10]

Palliative care is therefore a medical specialty that embodies a philosophy of care and a patient-centred care delivery model. It represents a valuable set of specialised services that complement continuous doctor-directed care aimed at providing disease modification therapy and comfort to the patient. Its primary focus is to prevent, diagnose, treat and reduce the severity of symptoms, as well as provide relief to patients suffering from serious or potentially fatal illness, while at the same time assisting patients and their families in the relevant decision-making process. However, the attention is not always centred on the physical needs of the patient; support for family issues and spiritual values also form a significant part of the holistic process in maintaining and improving the patient's quality of life. Palliative care aims to relieve suffering throughout the disease trajectory and is applicable to all forms of life-threatening illnesses. Consequently, it constitutes an extension of care that covers all stages of disease, including but not limited to the end-of-life phase.

1.2.3 Hospice Care

Historically, the term hospice care is the earliest to emerge among the other terms which form the subject matter of the current discussion. The word "hospice" is derived from the Latin *hospes*, which means "host". The origin of hospice dates back to Greek and Roman times where lodging and hospitality for travellers eventually evolved into a rudimentary asylum for the sick. In the Middle Ages, hospices functioned as transit shelters and hospitals for those travelling along trade and pilgrim routes in Europe and the Middle East.

The foundation of the modern hospice movement has its roots in the UK, pioneered by Dame Cicely Saunders who established St. Christopher's Hospice in 1967, the first hospice centre in London. Saunders formulated much of the philosophical framework of care that still forms the underlying principles of contemporary hospice. In her work, Saunders recognised that proper hospice care required the involvement of a skilled interdisciplinary team, effective symptom and pain management, treatment of the patient and family as a single unit of care and the implementation of a homecare and bereavement programme.

[9] National Institute for Clinical Excellence (2004), p. 20.

[10] Cherny (2003), p. 1335.

Hospice care is considered to be a subset of palliative care that focuses on patients with life-limiting illnesses who no longer seek curative interventions and delivers comfort care at the end of life while placing emphasis on the involvement of patients and families in the decision-making process. Its goal is to manage symptoms and provide pain relief, allowing patients to undergo the dying process with dignity within the comfort of their own homes. Lattanzi-Licht and Connor describe hospice as coordinated interdisciplinary programme of pain and symptom management that includes supportive services for terminally ill patients and their families.[11] It accordingly addresses the physical, emotional, social and spiritual needs of such patients and "is a return to a more human, oriented philosophy of care aimed at controlling symptoms and improving the quality of life for individuals with a terminal illness".[12]

Hospice programmes consist of a variety of services, ranging from nursing care, counselling and occupational therapy to medical supplies and equipment, which are carried out by an interdisciplinary team of health and social care professionals. Although most hospice care are home-based, it also takes place in other settings such as nursing and residential care facilities and inpatient hospice units or acute care sectors in hospitals.

1.2.4 The Correlation Between "Supportive Care, "Palliative Care", "Hospice Care" and "End-of-Life Care"

There appear to be overlapping similarities between the terms "supportive care", "palliative care" and "hospice care". The most salient common denominator is that all three philosophies and models of care incorporate a holistic approach and support system tending to the physical, emotional, psychosocial and spiritual needs of patients and families, which are correspondingly aimed at optimising quality of life. Further, they involve the mobilisation of an interdisciplinary team of professionals such as doctors, nurses, psychologists, therapists, chaplains and social workers to render a range of services.

Supportive care, palliative care and hospice care however contain distinct features in their respective scopes of services. Palliative care seeks to control and reduce the severity of symptoms for patients who are seriously ill and can be delivered along with curative treatment at any time during the disease trajectory. It is accordingly relevant in both acute and long-term settings and is not only reserved for patients nearing the end of life. In this respect, palliative care ostensibly bears resemblance to the elements of supportive care. Davis and Kuebler note that these two forms of care are dependent on one another and are equally important in delivering an optimal and comprehensive healthcare regime.[13] Supportive care is more encompassing in that it covers a wide range of issues from survivorship to

[11] See Lattanzi-Licht and Connor (1995), p. 143.

[12] Lattanzi-Licht and Connor (1995), p. 143.

[13] See Davis and Kuebler (2007), p. 25.

bereavement throughout the patient pathway. Although it does not constitute a distinct specialty, supportive care is the collective responsibility of all personnel specialising in social and healthcare. Thus, while supportive care is integrated in all palliative programmes, not all supportive care is palliative in nature.

While hospice care forms a part of palliative care, these two terms are not be used interchangeably. Hospice care differs from palliative care in terms of the timeframe in which it takes place, i.e. when patients enter into the final stages of their lives. In addition, curative treatment no longer forms part of the process, and the delivery of services are carried out for the most part, in a community setting. Therefore, palliative care may not necessarily involve hospice care as not all clinical modalities of palliative care are provided within the hospice system.

Based on the above discussion, it may be deduced that hospice care is a subdivision of palliative care and palliative care accordingly falls under supportive care which constitutes the "umbrella" term. Accordingly, end-of-life care falls within the spectrum of palliative care, which, as a matter of course, entails the delivery of hospice services. ESMO defines "end-of-life care" as palliative care that is delivered when death is imminent. According to the US National Quality Forum, end-of-life care applies when a patient's chronic illness is no longer curable and life-prolonging therapies are no longer appropriate indicated or desired. It refers to "a specific phase of palliative care requiring specialised skills and services that may be served by the delivery of hospice care or other models of palliative care programmes".[14]

While end-of-life care is a part of the broad dimension of palliative care, the latter on the hand is not confined to and does not axiomatically indicate end-of-life care. In this respect, the objection raised by some authors that "end-of-life care" is a misnomer in depicting the factual clinical practices of palliative care is therefore not without warrant. Nevertheless, while "end-of-life care" should not be used interchangeably with "palliative care", this does not negate the significance of the former term in referring to care of the terminally ill. As indicated by Kinzbrunner, the term "end-of-life care" is applied in a considerable amount of medical literature, and this he suggests is a valid descriptor to characterise care delivered in the final phase of life.[15] To this end, it serves to distinguish between two categories of patients receiving palliative care: those who are terminally ill and those who are not.

1.3 Scope of End-of-Life Decisions

Due to its nature, issues in end-of-life care inevitably revolve around the terminally ill patient's quality of life, the dying process and ultimately death. In the modern healthcare setting, death is no longer a definitive matter; pharmacological

[14] National Quality Forum (2006), p. C-2. In the USA, hospice care under the Medicare hospice benefit programme is provided to terminally ill patients whose prognosis of life expectancy is six months or less.

[15] See Kinzbrunner (2005), p. 5.

breakthroughs and advances in technology with regard to life-prolonging therapy and other medical interventions have blurred the lines between life and death. Patients who are on life support, for example, are able to live longer, despite no longer possessing cognitive and sensory functions. Thus, end-of-life issues relate to matters of consideration in the decision-making process in respect of clinical practices and procedures that could lead to the death of a terminally ill patient. Consequently, euthanasia emerges as a fundamentally relevant issue to be discussed vis-à-vis the context of such medical actions. It is therefore necessary to look into these aspects prior to examining the factors and considerations that impact upon the decisions made on treatment options for patients suffering from life-limiting illnesses, commonly referred to as end-of-life decisions.

1.3.1 Euthanasia

Literally, the word *euthanasia* means "good death" as derived from two Greek words *eu* which means well or good and *thanatos* which means death. The *Oxford English Dictionary* defines euthanasia as "the painless killing of a patient suffering from an incurable and painful disease or in an irreversible coma". From the healthcare perspective, euthanasia means the intentional putting to death of a person with an incurable or painful disease intended as an act of mercy. It is also seen as "the implementation of a decision that a particular individual's life will come to an end before it need to do so—a decision that life will end when it could be prolonged".[16] The European Association for Palliative Care (EAPC) adopts the position that euthanasia is killing upon request and describes it as "[a] doctor intentionally killing a person by the administration of drugs, at that person's voluntary and competent request".[17] In the legal context, euthanasia contemplates a medical practitioner causing the death of a patient whose terminal illness is the source of unbearable pain and distress.

Euthanasia can be further classified into the following categories: active euthanasia, passive euthanasia, voluntary euthanasia, nonvoluntary euthanasia and involuntary euthanasia.

1.3.1.1 Active Euthanasia

Active euthanasia occurs whenever positive and deliberate steps are taken which result in death such as injecting a lethal dose of medication into the patient. Another form of active euthanasia is assisted suicide or assisted dying, where the doctor assists the patient to bring about his or her death. The difference between active

[16] Harris (1997), p. 6.

[17] Materstvedt et al. (2003), p. 98.

euthanasia and assisted dying lies in the person who commits the last act which causes death; in cases of active euthanasia, this act is performed by the doctor, while in an assisted dying, it is the patient himself.

1.3.1.2 "Passive Euthanasia"

"Passive euthanasia" occurs where available measures to prolong life are withheld or withdrawn or, in other words, no positive action is taken to extend the life of a terminally ill patient. This includes not commencing treatment if it is considered futile and will not help to improve the patient's condition, disconnecting life support systems, discontinuing medical treatment necessary to sustain life or withholding supply of fluids and nutritional feeding. While active euthanasia is executed by an act, "passive euthanasia" is usually carried out by omission.

The use of the term "passive euthanasia" in referring to withdrawal and withholding of medical interventions, however, has been the subject of much debate among experts. The main contention is that there are appropriate circumstances in which withdrawal or withholding treatment is completely ethical and constitutes proper medical practice (e.g. in the case of futile treatment or when the patient refuses treatment), and therefore it would be inaccurate and misleading to describe such medical action as passive euthanasia. Garrard and Wilkinson aver that three conditions need to be fulfilled in the case of "passive euthanasia": (1) there is a withdrawing or withholding of life-prolonging treatment; (2) the main purpose (or one of the main purposes) of the withdrawing or withholding is to bring about (or "hasten") the patient's death; and (3) the reason for "hastening" death is that dying (or dying sooner rather than later) is in the patient's own best interests.[18] Thus, according to them, not all situations of withdrawal or withholding of treatment fall within the ambit of "passive euthanasia", as such medical action may not necessarily be undertaken with the intention to end the patient's life. This accords with Keown's view that "passive euthanasia" indicates the intentional hastening of the patient's death by withholding or withdrawing treatment, where causing death is the doctor's aim.[19] He further elaborates that "[p]assive euthanasia is not stopping treatments the doctor thinks worthless, but about stopping lives the doctor thinks worthless". Consequently, passive euthanasia would only form a subset under the spectrum of withdrawal or withholding of treatment. The EAPC go further as to dismiss the validity of the term; it opines that since "euthanasia" itself is active by definition, "passive euthanasia" is therefore an oxymoron and should not be used. As a result, many scholars now avoid using the term "passive euthanasia" in their writings and discussions.

---

[18] See Garrard and Wilkinson (2005), p. 65.

[19] Keown (2003), p. 462.

Nevertheless, some writers are of the view that in spite of the concern raised pertaining to the concept of "passive euthanasia", it need not be entirely abandoned provided that it is properly and narrowly defined and that cases of withdrawal and withholding of treatment that involve a direct intention to cause death are distinguished from cases where such an intention is absent. Garrard and Wilkinson, for instance, argue that "passive euthanasia" when assigned the correct connotation "is a useful expression and one which healthcare professionals should be allowed to employ in their discussions of policy and clinical practice".[20]

In view of the preceding contentions, due to the definitional complexity and in order to cautiously avert any confusion, the term "withdrawal or withholding of treatment" (and their linguistic derivations) will be used to indicate the foregoing of life-sustaining treatments that are likely to shorten the patient's life, but are not carried out with the intention to put an end to it. "Passive euthanasia", on the other hand, will specifically refer to withdrawal or withholding of treatment that is intentionally done to cause the patient's death. It is submitted that by selecting such preference, this will in turn facilitate the subsequent discussions on the distinction between "killing" and "letting die" and issues on the legalisation of active voluntary euthanasia.

1.3.1.3 Voluntary Euthanasia, Nonvoluntary Euthanasia and Involuntary Euthanasia

"Voluntary euthanasia" refers to a situation when euthanasia is requested and consented to by a competent patient. On the other hand, if euthanasia is conducted on a person who is unable to express an opinion due to lack of capacity to do so, for example, an insensate patient, this amounts to "nonvoluntary euthanasia". In such a case, it is usually the patient's family members and relatives who will consider whether it would be in accordance with the patient's wishes and in his best interests for steps to be taken to end his life. The difference between "nonvoluntary euthanasia" and "involuntary euthanasia' is that in the case of the latter, the termination of life is carried out against the will or without the consent of a competent patient. It also includes situations where the person has expressed a wish to the contrary.

1.3.2 Assisted Suicide or Assisted Dying

Assisted suicide or assisted dying is used to describe the situation where a doctor, at the patient's voluntary and competent request, intentionally provides the means to end the patient's life by providing lethal drugs which the patient self-administers. The distinction between assisted dying and euthanasia is the degree of the doctor's

[20] Garrard and Wilkinson (2005), p. 68.

participation in the act. As previously explained, in euthanasia, it is the doctor who administers the fatal substance, which may be in the form of a lethal injection. In the case of assisted dying, the doctor assists the patient to end his life by prescribing the medication that would serve such purpose; he may or may not be present when the patient undertakes the final act. Some suggest that that assisted dying is morally preferable and affords a more autonomous way for a patient to end his life compared to euthanasia, since the patient has more control over the immediate life-ending act which allows him to change his mind up about his decision up to the very last minute. However, there is the possibility that assisted dying may turn into euthanasia when the patient is unable to complete the process of ending his life. For example, the patient may be unable to properly ingest the lethal medication and require direct assistance from the doctor. Although assisted dying is considered by many to be in violation of the traditional prohibition against using the tools of medicine to end a life, some doctors believe it to the last act of compassion on a continuum of care for the terminally ill.

1.3.3 Withholding or Withdrawal of Treatment

The withholding or withdrawal of life-sustaining treatment is an issue frequently encountered in end-of-life care. There are several reasons for such interventions to be withheld or withdrawn; the first of which relates to the futility of treatment which can no longer achieve its intended goal and will not provide any therapeutic benefit to the patient. Medical futility is described as an intervention that will not be able to reach its intended goal. Doctors may also withhold or withdraw treatment that would inflict excessive burdens on the patient or when the treatment would result in unnecessary application of limited resources that would deprive others who are more in need. Another justification for withholding or withdrawing treatment is the refusal of the patient itself. Doctors must withhold or withdraw treatment when a competent patient refuses it or when a valid advance decision has been made in the case of a patient who lacks capacity. There is accordingly no moral or ethical distinction between withholding and withdrawing life-sustaining treatment.

Withholding or withdrawal of life-sustaining treatments includes but is not limited to the following medical actions:

(a) ***Cardiopulmonary resuscitation (CPR):*** This refers to the emergency medical protocol used in an attempt to restart breathing and blood circulation in a patient who suffers cardiopulmonary arrest. It increases a person's chance of surviving a sudden cardiac arrest. Patients who do not wish to receive CPR may request for a do-not-resuscitate (DNR) order from their doctor, which the latter has an obligation to honour. Situations where a DNR order might be issued are, among others, (i) when CPR may not provide benefit to the patient; (ii) administration of CPR would result in permanent damage or poor quality of life; or (iii) patients suffer from poor quality of life and wish to forego CPR in the case of cardiac arrest.

(b) ***Mechanical ventilation:*** Mechanical ventilation is a common treatment at the end of life and is the form of life support which is most frequently withheld or withdrawn in anticipation of death. It is provided by a ventilator that inflates and deflates the lungs to assist patients who are unable to properly breathe on their own. It may be delivered by way of intubation, i.e. through an endotracheal tube that is inserted into the mouth or nose, or tracheostomy, in which the tube is inserted through a surgical hole in the patient's neck.

(c) ***Artificial nutrition and hydration:*** These therapies provide nutrients and water to patients who are unconscious or unable to swallow. Artificial nutrients are administered through two methods: enteral feeding and intravenous feeding (or total parenteral nutrition). Enteral feeding requires the use of feeding tubes to deliver nutrients directly into a patient's stomach or intestines through several routes: nasogastric, gastrostomy, jejunostomy and esophagostomy. Intravenous feeding delivers nutrients directly into the bloodstream. Artificial fluid therapy is delivered via the following routes: intravenous, rectal or enteral. Dehydration at the end of life causes suffering to some patients, which are relieved by the administration of artificial nutrition and hydration. Although clinically and ethically, artificial nutrition is not differentiated from other life-sustaining treatments, the withholding or withdrawal of such intervention remains one of the most controversial issues in end-of-life care as it is identified with depriving people with their basic human needs of food and water.

1.3.4 Pain Management at the End of Life: Palliative and Terminal Sedation

Terminally ill patients at the end of life may experience severe symptoms such as dyspnoea, pain, delirium, restlessness and vomiting that are refractory, to which normal interventions provide no relief. In such cases, doctors may sedate the patient to a state of unconsciousness in order to alleviate the patient's intractable suffering and discomfort. This is known as palliative sedation. According to ESMO, palliative sedation is "the monitored use of medications intended to induce a state of decreased or absent awareness (unconsciousness) in order to relieve the burden of otherwise intractable suffering in a manner that is ethically acceptable to the patient, family and health-care providers".[21] According to Morita, the concept of sedation consists of two components: (1) the presence of intractable or severe distress refractory to standard palliative treatment and (2) the use of sedative medications with the primary aim of relieving severe symptoms by reducing consciousness.[22] It is to be

[21] Cherny and Radbruch (2009), p. 581.

[22] See Morita et al. (1999), p. 20.

differentiated with sedation that is administered prior to carrying out medical procedures such as intubation and the inadvertent sedative effects of pain relief medications or anaesthesia. According to the British Medical Association, it is ethical to deeply sedate a terminally ill or dying patient at the risk of hastening the patient's death when it is in the best interests of the patient to do so, the method of intervention forms part of proper medical practice and the purpose of the act is to relieve the patient's suffering.[23]

The traditional concern surrounding the use of high doses of opioids in the palliative care setting is that it causes respiratory depression which would hasten the death of the patient. The ethical justification for this finds its ground in the doctrine of double effect. Under this principle, an act that has both good and bad effect is ethically permissible if it fulfils the following conditions: (1) the act itself is good; (2) the act is performed with the intention of achieving the good effect without intending the bad effect, although the latter was foreseen prior to the act being undertaken; (3) the good effect is not obtained by means of the bad effect; and (4) there is a proportionately grave reason for permitting the bad effect. Palliative sedation fulfils the requirements in that (1) the administration of sedatives in itself is a good act as it is done with the aim of relieving pain or suffering, which is the good effect; (2) death being the bad effect, although foreseen, is not intended; (3) death is not the means to relief of pain or suffering; and (4) the principle of proportionality is exercised taking into consideration the condition, needs and consent of the patient.

There is broad consensus, however, that the notion that heavy sedation would accelerate the dying process of the terminally ill patients is unfounded and may have been overemphasised. Analyses conducted by experts provide evidence showing that there is little basis in the claim that administering opioid analgesics at the end of life shortens the lives of patients, thus lending credence to the argument that it is unnecessary to invoke the doctrine of double effect to justify palliative sedation.

Several terms have been used interchangeably with "palliative sedation", including "terminal sedation", "total sedation", "sedation in the terminal" or "final stages of life" and "palliation sedation therapy". The most contentious term, however, is "terminal sedation". It is to be noted that although palliative sedation in general does not shorten life, administering deep and continuous sedation while foregoing artificial nutrition and hydration from a terminally ill patient will hasten the patient's death. This is attributable to the effects of such sedation; it renders the patient incapable of interaction with others and the ability to eat and drink, and therefore a decision to withhold or withdraw artificial nutrition and hydration at the same time would necessarily result in hastening the patient's death. A number of authors agree that in such a case, death is accelerated by dehydration and starvation, rather than the underlying disease. Authors such as Quill, Battin and Marker refer to such practice as terminal sedation, in order to differentiate it with the relatively common practice of palliative sedation.[24] Battin further argues that the word "terminal"

[23] See British Medical Association Ethics Department (2012), p. 466.

[24] See Quill (2006), p. 577; Battin (2008), pp. 27–30; and Marker (2011), pp. 99–119.

indicates the foreseeability of death, which is the most significant element in the process of palliative sedation that includes the withholding or withdrawal of artificial nutrition and hydration, and to refrain from using it will cause confusion between such medical action with "palliative care".[25]

Thus, for purposes of connoting the difference between the two types of practices, palliative sedation which is accompanied by the withholding or withdrawal of artificial nutrition and hydration will be referred to as "terminal sedation". Due to the controversy surrounding the second component of terminal sedation, i.e. foregoing artificial nutrition and hydration, this has led to intense debates on the ethical justification of terminal sedation as a whole.

1.4 Development of Palliative Care in Malaysia

The first palliative care service in Malaysia finds its roots in the establishment of a hospice home care initiative by the Penang Cancer Society in 1991. In August of the same year, Hospis Malaysia was founded, a non-profit charitable organisation dedicated to providing professional palliative care services to those suffering from life-limiting illnesses. A few years later, other states such as Sabah, Malacca and Sarawak began to follow suit and offer hospice services. In 1995, the first hospital-based palliative care unit was set up in Queen Elizabeth Hospital, Kota Kinabalu. This development accordingly formed the catalyst which precipitated the expansion of palliative care services in the country.[26] Recognising the apparent need to provide continuous care to patients who were discharged from the inpatient unit, a collaborative network between the hospital's inpatient unit and volunteer-based home care programme began to develop, creating what is now termed as "seamless care".[27] Under this system, patients who have received palliative treatment at the hospital and are discharged would immediately be enrolled into the home care programme run by the Palliative Care Association of Kota Kinabalu to ensure that they are accorded continuous care and comfort. The practice works both ways; patients would consequently have a clear-cut access to the services of the palliative care unit in the event that medical attention or hospital admission is required. The positive outcome of this scheme of integrated care led to the issuance of a directive by the Ministry of Health ("MOH") in 1997, which instructed all state and district government hospitals to develop palliative care units by the year 2000, especially in hospitals providing specialist services to handle intricate disease processes involving patients with life-limiting illnesses.[28] In 1998, the Malaysian Hospice Council was established, which served as the umbrella body for hospice and palliative care

[25] See Battin (2008), p. 28.

[26] Lim (2003), p. 78.

[27] Lim (2003), p. 81.

[28] See Medical Development Division Ministry of Health Malaysia (1997).

organisations in Malaysia. As a result of the MOH directive, dedicated hospital-based palliative care units began to proliferate in hospitals across the country, and as a means to further promote the development and practice of palliative medicine among local healthcare professionals, the MOH recognised palliative medicine as a subspecialty in 2005.[29] Subsequently in 2010, an operational policy on palliative care services was issued by MOH's Medical Development Division, which aims to provide guidance to healthcare providers on the scope, components, training requirements and the types of palliative care services and organisational structures based on an integrated palliative care model which are to be carried out in collaboration with community-based centres.[30] This has since been replaced by the National Palliative Care: Policy and Strategic Plan 2019–2030.[31] The later policy and strategic plan marks a discernible shift in emphasis. Whereas the 2010 operational policy was primarily directed at setting out the scope of service, components of care, organisational structures and training requirements for service delivery, the 2019 document broadens the framework into a national roadmap anchored in universal health coverage, equity, continuity of care, workforce development, community participation and quality standards. It also places more express emphasis on strengthening domiciliary and community-based palliative care, collaboration with NGO hospices and the development of paediatric palliative care, thereby reflecting a more comprehensive and future-oriented policy framework for Malaysia.

Currently, palliative care in Malaysia is no longer discussed merely in terms of the availability of a limited number of hospital-based units, but increasingly in relation to the scale of national need, the integration of services across settings and the capacity of the health system to respond to an ageing population. Population-based modelling by Yang et al. demonstrates that adult palliative care needs rose from 71,675 cases in 2004 to 100,034 cases in 2014 and are projected to reach at least 239,713 cases by 2030.[32] This projected increase is especially significant among older adults aged 80 years and above and underscores that the need for palliative care in Malaysia is not static but is expected to expand at a pace that may outstrip existing service provision unless integration and workforce development are correspondingly strengthened.

More recent developments indicate that palliative care has begun to receive greater policy recognition within wider health system reform. The Health White Paper for Malaysia expressly situates palliative care within the continuum of comprehensive, person-centred primary healthcare and envisages the delivery of more care closer to the community and home settings.[33] This is complemented by the publication of Advance Care Planning: A Guide for Healthcare Practitioners in Malaysia in 2024 ("ACP Guide"), which constitutes an important step towards

[29] See Wright et al. (2010), pp. 34–37.

[30] See Medical Development Division Ministry of Health Malaysia (2010), p. 21.

[31] Medical Development Division Ministry of Health Malaysia (2019).

[32] See Yang et al. (2020), pp. e129–e136.

[33] See Ministry of Health Malaysia (2023).

structured communication on patients' preferences, although advance care planning in Malaysia remains at a relatively early stage and is not yet supported by a comprehensive legal framework.[34] At the same time, recent local studies continue to identify substantial disparities in geographical accessibility, particularly between the Central Region, the East Coast and East Malaysia, as well as persistent gaps in training among primary care physicians and the need for better quality indicators to evaluate end-of-life care delivery.[35] These findings suggest that while Malaysia has made notable progress, the present challenge lies less in recognising the importance of palliative care than in ensuring equitable access, adequate expertise and consistent standards of practice throughout the country.

1.5 Socioreligious Context of End-of-Life Care in Malaysia

Religion and spirituality, through social support and coping mechanisms, enhance a patient's well-being and substantially mediate quality of life. Since clinical assessments on a patient's quality of life involve an insight into physical, social and psychological aspects, the inclusion of measures of religiosity and spirituality into the medical framework will facilitate doctors towards a better understanding of patients' beliefs, values, expectations and needs and at the same time facilitate a dynamic interaction between patients, family members and healthcare professionals. The management and delivery of end-of-life care, particularly in a pluralistic society, must therefore necessarily rely on sociocultural influences, apart from clinical and ethical considerations.

The ignorance and lack of sensitivity in understanding and appreciating the different religious and cultural attitudes towards death and the dying process constitute a barrier towards effective communication between doctor and patient and the provision of competent end-of-life care. Difficulties may occur in cases where there exists conflict between religious and cultural values of the patient and that of routine medical practice. Ethical dilemmas may also arise when a doctor's own set of values are unfamiliar to and inconsistent with the patient's personal beliefs. In non-Western cultures, particularly Asian communities, patient autonomy is approached differently, and the degree of emphasis placed on the principle is less than the current medical norm in the West. Family members play a more dominant role than the patient in the decision-making process; they prefer to be the first point of contact to be fully informed of the patient's condition and then conclude as to how much disclosure is to be relayed to the latter. This is done as an effort to shield the patient from information that might be disrespectful or disturbing, which may cause the patient mental anxiety and adversely affect his or her will to live. The notion that it

[34] See Lim et al. (2023), pp. 103–106, Ministry of Health and Advance Care Planning Guidance Working Group (2024), and Nalliah et al. (2021), pp. 279–283.

[35] See Hamdan et al. (2023), p. 550; Segarmurthy et al. (2024), pp. 255–263; and Wong et al. (2025), p. 311.

is the family who shoulders the responsibility of receiving bad news and making difficult end-of-life decisions is prevalent in Asian cultures which are typically family-centred.

In Malaysia, where cultural and religious diversity deeply influences healthcare practices, the role of the family remains particularly pronounced and often mediates the manner in which patients articulate or defer treatment preferences. Recent Malaysian studies further suggest that spirituality continues to function as a significant source of emotional strength and preparedness in the face of poor prognosis and dying. In a qualitative study involving Malaysian patients with advanced cancer, spirituality was identified as one of the principal factors shaping how patients coped with serious illness and engaged with discussions on future care.[36] Likewise, recent work on Christian family caregivers in Malaysia illustrates how prayer, emotional accompaniment and the preservation of hope form an integral part of the care process while at the same time revealing the practical difficulty of meeting spiritual needs in settings where resources and formal guidance remain limited.[37]

Accordingly, patients from certain cultural backgrounds may hold different perspectives on pain and suffering at the end of life. Although it is the doctor's duty to ensure that the patient is accorded as much relief and comfort as possible in the final stages of his illness, some terminally ill patients may view suffering as a necessary means to achieve a dignified end and a better afterlife and therefore choose to refuse heavy sedation so that they can maintain a high level of consciousness until death takes place. In such cases, it is important for healthcare professionals to recognise the religious importance of such preferences and adequately address them. Such challenges may further be compounded by the inability of healthcare institutions to accommodate the diverse religious and cultural needs of patients due to a paucity of sufficient resources. Most institutions, due to the lack of facilities and trained personnel, are only able to implement "a one-size-fits-all" care system, which may hinder the capacity to adjust services to suit a patient's cultural preferences.

In view of the above, there is a need for doctors to recognise the way in which different religious and ethnic groups perceive the information relating to their prognosis and treatment, as well as the reasons that frame their responses in relation to the decision-making process. Cultural competence, which enhances the organisation of culturally effective care in a clinical environment, therefore requires not only skilful verbal and non-verbal communication but also an institutional willingness to incorporate spiritual and family-centred concerns into end-of-life discussions. This has now begun to receive greater formal recognition in local guidance, particularly through the ACP Guide, which encourages clinicians to explore patients' values, beliefs and preferences as part of shared decision-making.[38] Better healthcare especially at the end of life can only be achieved if these factors are given due

---

[36] See Chung et al. (2025), pp. 85–93.

[37] See Mohamad Ismail et al. (2025), pp. 86–97.

[38] See Ministry of Health and Advance Care Planning Guidance Working Group (2024).

consideration, as medicine does not merely deal with elements of pure science but also major and intrinsic humanistic and ethical components.

1.5.1 Religious Demography in Malaysia

An analysis of religious considerations regarding end-of-life decisions in the context of Malaysian medical practice must necessarily take into account the values and perspectives of the different communities which make up Malaysia's ethno-cultural demography. Malays constitute the largest ethnic group in Malaysia, comprising 58.1% of the entire population, followed by Chinese (23.2%), Indians (6.7%) and others (0.7%).[39] Although religious faiths are not necessarily identified according to the respective ethnic groups, Malays are ordinarily identified as Muslims. Under article 160 of the Malaysian Federal Constitution, "Malay" means "a person who professes the religion of Islam, habitually speaks the Malay language, conforms to Malay custom and (a) was before Merdeka Day born in the Federation or in Singapore or born of parents one of whom was born in the Federation or in Singapore or is on that day domiciled in the Federation or in Singapore or (b) is the issue of such a person". Islam as the principal and official religion in Malaysia[40] accounts for 63.5%, and Buddhism constitutes the second largest religion with 18.7%, while Christianity and Hinduism comprise 9.1% and 6.1%, respectively (see Fig. 1.1).[41]

Accordingly, religious stances have always been an important and influential factor in the advancement of policy and regulatory frameworks in Malaysia. Although the provisions of the Federal Constitution do not explicitly require that legislation must be in conformity with any particular set of religious principles, the constitutional guarantee and protection accorded to religious practices[42] and the influence of

[39] Department of Statistics Malaysia (2025). The Population and Housing Census is undertaken every 10 years.

[40] See Article 3 of the Federal Constitution.

[41] Department of Statistics Malaysia (2025). Figure generated by ChatGPT Plus.

[42] Apart from Article 3, Article 11 of the Federal Constitution provides for religious freedom. The provision states:

"(1) Every person has the right to profess and practise his religion and, subject to Clause (4), to propagate it.

(2) No person shall be compelled to pay any tax the proceeds of which are specially allocated in whole or in part for the purposes of a religion other than his own.

(3) Every religious group has the right—

(a) to manage its own religious affairs;

(b) to establish and maintain institutions for religious or charitable purposes; and

(c) to acquire and own property and hold and administer it in accordance with law.

(4) State law and in respect of the Federal Territories of Kuala Lumpur, Labuan and Putrajaya, federal law may control or restrict the propagation of any religious doctrine or belief among persons professing the religion of Islam.

(5) This Article does not authorize any act contrary to any general law relating to public order, public health or morality".

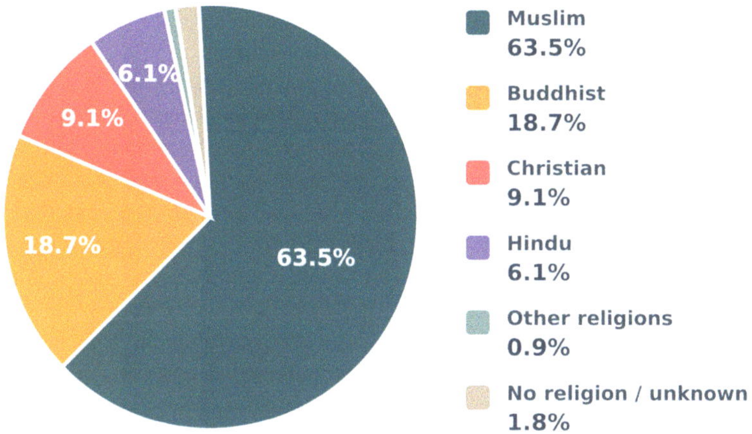

Fig. 1.1 Percentage distribution of the Malaysian population by religion

religious ideals in the lawmaking process in Malaysia are evidences of the impact that religion has on the country's legal development. Islamic influence, in particular, has played a significant role in the construction of the social and political affairs of the country.

1.5.2 Religious Guidance on End-of-Life Decisions

The religious guidance on end-of-life decisions in Malaysia is necessarily informed by the fact that Islam is the religion of the Federation and the faith professed by the majority of the population, while Buddhism, Christianity and Hinduism continue to shape the moral outlook of sizeable segments of Malaysian society. Across these traditions, the most consistent point of convergence is the recognition that human life is sacred and may not be intentionally terminated. Accordingly, active euthanasia and assisted dying remain morally unacceptable from the perspective of the major religions practised in Malaysia, even if compassion for suffering is emphasised within each tradition.

From the Islamic perspective, the prohibition against active euthanasia is anchored in the doctrine of sanctity of life and the understanding that life and death ultimately belong to Allah. Islamic guidance, however, does not require life to be prolonged by all possible means regardless of clinical benefit. Where treatment is assessed by the appropriate medical experts to be futile and no longer conducive to recovery, withholding or withdrawing such treatment may be permissible, provided that the intention is not to cause death but to refrain from non-beneficial intervention. The Malaysian position reflected in national and state fatwa deliberations is broadly consistent with this approach while continuing to place significant weight on expert medical opinion and collective decision-making.

This position is also reflected, albeit in more practical clinical terms, in the recent ACP Guide, which recognises that Muslim patients may refuse treatment where its efficacy is doubtful or its burden excessive, but not where the refusal is intended to hasten death.[43] At the same time, Islamic discourse continues to exhibit caution in relation to artificial nutrition and hydration, which are frequently treated as supportive care that ought, in principle, to be maintained even after definitive treatment is withdrawn. This remains one of the areas in which medico-clinical assessments and religious expectations may not always neatly coincide.

More specifically, Islamic religious edicts and professional ethical guidance draw a clear distinction between positive acts intended to end life and the clinical decision to refrain from futile intervention. Religious edicts issued by Islamic authorities, and the Islamic Code of Medical and Health Ethics, prohibit active euthanasia and assisted dying because human life is regarded as sacred and the doctor's role is not to terminate it.[44]

At the same time, Islamic guidance does not insist that life be prolonged by futile or non-beneficial treatment at all costs. On the local front, Malaysian fatwa guidance similarly permits the discontinuation of primary or curative treatment in situations of medical futility while emphasising professional assessment, multidisciplinary deliberation and discussion with the patient's family.[45] The withholding or withdrawal of life-sustaining treatment may be permissible where suitably qualified medical experts determine that further intervention is futile and recovery is no longer anticipated, the intention being not to cause death but to refrain from non-beneficial treatment. This emphasis on professional assessment resonates with the reliance placed in Islamic discourse on *ahl al-khibrah*, or expert medical opinion. Further, Islamic guidance on pain management at the end of life recognises that the administration of analgesia for the purpose of alleviating suffering is not to be equated with euthanasia merely because death may foreseeably ensue, so long as the intention remains therapeutic rather than to hasten death.[46] Islamic guidance also exhibits a careful distinction between definitive treatment and supportive care. While palliative measures aimed at relieving suffering are generally acceptable, there remains a strong tendency to maintain basic care, especially nutrition and hydration, until death occurs naturally. Such guidance reinforces the broader point that the permissibility of end-of-life decisions in Islam turns not only on outcome but also on intention, clinical benefit and the nature of the intervention withheld.

A synthesis of the other major religious perspectives in Malaysia reveals a notable degree of normative overlap. Buddhist, Christian and Hindu teachings, notwithstanding their doctrinal differences, similarly reject the deliberate taking of life and

[43] See Ministry of Health and Advance Care Planning Guidance Working Group (2024).

[44] IMANA Ethics Committee (2005) and Islamic Organization for Medical Sciences (2005).

[45] Jabatan Mufti Negeri Selangor (2023) and Jawatankuasa Fatwa Negeri Perak (2018).

[46] Jawatankuasa Fatwa Negeri Perak (2018).

uphold compassion, dignity and moral responsibility in the care of the dying. Yet none of these traditions insist that life be prolonged at all costs by aggressive measures that are futile and excessively burdensome or merely postpone an inevitable death. In this respect, the major faiths in Malaysia converge more closely on the impermissibility of intentional killing than they diverge on the permissibility of foregoing non-beneficial treatment.

Within Buddhism, the moral gravity of intention is particularly significant. Compassion towards the suffering patient is central, but intentional killing remains wrongful because it interferes with karma and the moral consequences of death. At the same time, Buddhist perspectives do not ordinarily require the use or continuation of futile treatment where death is imminent. Another recurring theme is the importance of mental clarity and a peaceful state of mind at the end of life, which explains why some Buddhist patients may be cautious about deep sedation if it impedes awareness, prayer or meditative composure.

Christian perspectives similarly place strong emphasis on the sanctity of life, human dignity and the duty to care for the vulnerable. Active euthanasia and assisted dying are generally rejected, but Christian ethical thought has long drawn a distinction between intentionally causing death and foregoing disproportionate or extraordinary means of treatment. Thus, withholding or withdrawing treatment that offers no reasonable hope of benefit may be morally acceptable, while pain relief and palliative sedation are usually justified where the intention is to alleviate suffering rather than to end life. Recent Malaysian research on Christian family caregivers also demonstrates that prayer, emotional presence and the sustaining of hope remain central features of end-of-life care within Christian families.[47]

Hindu perspectives, much like Buddhist thought, are influenced by ideas of karma, suffering and the spiritual significance of the dying process. Life is to be treated with reverence, and active euthanasia is generally impermissible, yet futile prolongation of dying is not favoured. Hindu patients may attach particular importance to consciousness, prayer, ritual observance and family presence when approaching death, and this may affect their views on sedation, artificial feeding and the timing of treatment limitation. Recent literature reviewing Hindu family caregiving in palliative contexts further underscores the role of spiritual preparation, ritual continuity and family obligation in shaping end-of-life preferences.[48]

What emerges from the foregoing is that religious guidance in the Malaysian context should not be treated as peripheral to clinical decision-making, but as one of its material constituents. The principal implication for healthcare providers is not that every patient will adhere rigidly to a singular doctrinal position but that religious beliefs may shape attitudes towards prognosis disclosure, shared decision-making, pain management, sedation and the withholding or withdrawal of treatment. Accordingly, any attempt to formulate a coherent Malaysian framework on end-of-life decisions must be attentive not only to Islamic principles but also to the broader

[47] See Mohamad Ismail et al. (2025), pp. 86–97.

[48] See Mohamad Ismail et al. (2024), pp. 188–209.

multi-faith moral landscape within which medical practice in Malaysia is carried out.

1.6 Relevance of Common Law in the Malaysian Legal System

Malaysia, having been under British colonial rule in the nineteenth and twentieth centuries, inherits much of its legal system from the common law in England. The prevailing influence of the laws of England is codified in Section 3 of the Civil Law Act 1956, which provides for the application of the common law of England and rules of equity, subject to specified cut-off dates and to the qualification that such principles are only to be received so far as local circumstances permit.[49] This statutory mechanism has historically operated as the principal avenue through which common law reasoning entered the Malaysian legal system and continues to explain why English authorities remain highly persuasive in areas where local legislation is silent or underdeveloped.

The strict application of section 3, however, does not by itself resolve the regulatory gap on end-of-life decisions in Malaysia. The difficulty lies not only in the antiquity of the cut-off dates but also in the impracticality of attempting to freeze the common law at a historical moment when the law in England has since evolved through later judicial and statutory developments. As observed by former Chief Justice Tun Abdul Hamid Mohamad in calling for a review of the Act, Malaysian judges have in reality "hardly take the trouble to determine the common law or the rules of equity as at the cut-off date", and English judgments are frequently cited as though Section 3 did not exist.[50] The significance of this observation is that current English common law continues, in practical terms, to function as an important persuasive source in resolving novel medicolegal questions.

The influence of common law is particularly evident in the development of Malaysian medical law, where liability and professional responsibility have largely

[49] Section 3(1) of the Civil Law Act 1956 (Act 67) states:

"(1) Save so far as other provision has been made or may hereafter be made by any written law in force in Malaysia, the Court shall:

(a) in Peninsular Malaysia or any part thereof, apply the common law of England and the rules of equity as administered in England on the 7 April 1956;

(b) in Sabah, apply the common law of England and the rules of equity, together with statutes of general application, as administered or in force in England on 1 December 1951;

(c) in Sarawak, apply the common law of England and the rules of equity, together with statutes of general application, as administered or in force in England on 12 December 1949, subject however to subparagraph (3) (ii):

Provided always that the said common law, rules of equity and statutes of general application shall be applied so far only as the circumstances of the States of Malaysia and their respective inhabitants permit and subject to such qualifications as local circumstances render necessary".

[50] See Mohamad (2013).

evolved through common law negligence principles. Questions relating to duty of care, the standard of care, causation, consent and disclosure have been elaborated through judicial adoption and adaptation of English and other Commonwealth authorities. This is especially important in the present context because Malaysia still lacks a comprehensive statutory framework specifically governing end-of-life decisions, with the result that courts and practitioners must necessarily draw upon broader common law doctrines when addressing treatment limitation, autonomy and professional obligations.

The classic illustration of common law influence is the *Bolam*[51] test, which for many years shaped the assessment of medical negligence in Malaysia. Under this test, a doctor would not be regarded as negligent if he or she had acted in accordance with a practice accepted as proper by a responsible body of medical practitioners skilled in that particular field. This professional-centred approach was later qualified by *Bolitho*,[52] where the court affirmed the relevance of responsible medical opinion but held that such opinion must nevertheless be capable of withstanding logical analysis. In Malaysia, these principles continue to inform the assessment of negligence in matters concerning diagnosis and treatment. The development of local medical law, however, has not been confined to English authorities alone. In *Foo Fio Na v Dr Soo Fook Mun & Anor*,[53] the Federal Court moved away from a purely professional-centred approach in matters of disclosure and placed greater emphasis on the patient's right to be informed. This approach is consistent with the reasoning in *Rogers v Whitaker*,[54] where the duty to disclose material risks was assessed by reference to what a reasonable patient in the patient's position would consider significant, rather than solely by reference to what a responsible body of doctors would disclose. Later Malaysian decisions have accordingly clarified that while *Bolam*, as qualified by *Bolitho*, continues to govern diagnosis and treatment, the duty to advise patients of material risks is approached in a more patient-centred manner.[55] This development illustrates that Malaysian medical negligence law has drawn from both English and Australian common law principles in shaping the applicable standards of care.

This trajectory is significant for end-of-life decision-making, because the relevant legal questions extend beyond technical negligence in treatment and encompass matters of informed consent, refusal of treatment, best interests and the limits of professional discretion. The common law provides the conceptual tools through which these questions have historically been analysed, whether by distinguishing acts from omissions, scrutinising the reasonableness of continuing non-beneficial treatment or protecting patient autonomy in the face of medical paternalism.

---

[51] *Bolam v Friern Hospital Management Committee* [1957] 1 W.L.R. 582.

[52] *Bolitho v City and Hackney Health Authority* [1998] A.C. 232.

[53] *Foo Fio Na v Dr Soo Fook Mun and Assunta Hospital* [2007] 1 MLJ 593.

[54] *Rogers v Whitaker* (1992) 175 CLR 479.

[55] See, for instance, *Zulhasnimar bt Hasan Basri & Anor v Dr Kuppu Velumani P & Ors* [2017] 5 MLJ 438.

These developments illustrate that the relevance of common law in the Malaysian legal system lies not in the uncritical reception of English or Australian principles but in their careful adaptation to local circumstances. This is consistent with the proviso to Section 3 of the Civil Law Act 1956, which requires the common law of England to be applied only so far as the circumstances of Malaysia and its inhabitants permit. The qualification is especially significant in the context of end-of-life care, where legal analysis cannot be detached from Malaysia's religious demography, family-centred decision-making practices and healthcare realities. Thus, while the legal developments in common law jurisdictions such as England and Australia remain instructive, their principles must be examined with due regard to the Malaysian statutory framework, social context and normative considerations.

1.7 Overview of the Book

This chapter lays down the conceptual and contextual foundation for the discussion by clarifying the meaning and scope of end-of-life care and its relationship with supportive care, palliative care and hospice care. It then identifies the principal medical decisions that arise at the end of life, including active euthanasia, assisted dying, withholding and withdrawal of life-sustaining treatment and pain management through palliative or terminal sedation. The chapter further situates these issues within the Malaysian context by examining the development of palliative care services, the significance of religion and spirituality and the role of family involvement in the decision-making process.

Chapter 2 proceeds to examine the ethical dimensions of end-of-life decisions and the manner in which these ethical principles are reflected in Malaysian professional ethical guidance. It considers the application of the principles of sanctity of life, beneficence, non-maleficence, autonomy and justice and the manner in which these principles may come into tension in clinical practice. In particular, it discusses the ethical difficulties that arise where the duty to preserve life must be balanced against the obligation to relieve suffering, where patient autonomy is affected by questions of capacity or family disagreement and where limited healthcare resources require difficult decisions to be made. The chapter further considers the role of shared decision-making and examines Malaysian ethical codes, professional standards and clinical guidance insofar as they give practical expression to these ethical principles in local end-of-life care.

Chapter 3 then considers common law principles on end-of-life decisions and their relevance to unresolved questions within the Malaysian legal framework. This discussion is undertaken against the backdrop of the existing lacuna in Malaysian law, where no specific statutory provisions or local judicial decisions have yet set out a clear body of principles governing end-of-life medical decisions. Given the persuasive relevance of common law principles in areas where local law remains undeveloped, the experiences of the UK and Australia provide useful points of reference. The discussion does not suggest that these principles should be applied in Malaysia without due regard to local circumstances. Rather, the common law experience is examined for the guidance it may offer in clarifying the distinction between active life-ending acts, withholding and withdrawal of treatment, best interests, advance medical directives and palliative measures that may foreseeably hasten death.

Chapter 4 examines the statutory and regulatory position on end-of-life decisions in Malaysia by considering the relevant Penal Code provisions, professional ethical codes, clinical guidelines and palliative care standards. Although Malaysia does not yet have specific legislation governing end-of-life decision-making, the position is not entirely without guidance. Recent developments, including the ACP Guide, the revised Consent for Treatment of Patients by Registered Medical Practitioners issued by the Malaysian Medical Council, national palliative care standards and ongoing discussions on mental capacity reform, indicate a gradual movement towards a more patient-centred and professionally structured approach. Nevertheless, their largely non-statutory nature means that important aspects of end-of-life decision-making remain insufficiently settled in law.

Chapter 5 concludes the discussion by drawing together the central findings of the book and advancing the argument for building a coherent ethico-legal framework on end-of-life decisions in Malaysia. It reassesses the adequacies and inadequacies of the current Malaysian position, situates end-of-life care within the wider continuum of palliative care and identifies future reform priorities. These include the consolidation of professional guidance, the integration of religious and cultural considerations, clearer legal safeguards for doctors, the regulation of advance care planning and advance medical directives and service strategies that promote equitable access to palliative and end-of-life care. The chapter argues that professional guidance and legal reform should be developed in tandem, in a manner that remains attentive to Malaysia's legal order, professional realities and plural social fabric.

1.8 Conclusion

End-of-life care constitutes a component at the far end of the broad spectrum of palliative care, which focuses on delivering holistic care and support to terminally ill patients and their families. When such patients enter the final stages of their lives and life-sustaining treatment is no longer indicated or desired, this entails the provision of hospice care which seeks to afford comfort and optimise their quality of life until the final moment when death naturally takes place, as well as providing bereavement support for the families in the aftermath. A range of services are offered in end-of-life care, which are carried out by a multidisciplinary and interdisciplinary team of experts, comprising, among others, doctors, nurses, psychologists, therapists, nutritionists, chaplains and social workers. This is performed for the purpose of tending to the physical, emotional, psychosocial and spiritual needs of terminally ill patients as well as families. Medical actions undertaken in end-of-life care are consistently aimed at providing relief from pain and suffering, and in some cases, this may result in hastening the death of the patient. Thus, this raises the issue of whether such practices fall within the ambit of euthanasia. While assisted dying clearly amounts to active euthanasia as it involves an active and deliberate conduct with the express intention of ending the patient's life, there is a continuous debate on whether the withholding and withdrawal of life-sustaining treatment, which is often referred to as "letting die", is to be considered in the same light. Most experts maintain that there is a clear distinction between the two types of medical action and primarily rest their arguments on two principles: an omission to stop a person from dying cannot be treated as the moral equivalent of to actively kill a person and the doctrine of double effect. When a doctor withholds or withdraws treatment, the intention is to relieve the patient's suffering, rather than to cause the death of the patient; thus, in such a case, death is a foreseeable side effect, as opposed to active euthanasia, where death constitutes the means. Although the distinction may be subtle in the case of terminal sedation, it is argued that it remains ethically significant, since death is brought upon by the underlying illness from which the patient suffers from, and not due to the act of withdrawing artificial nutrition and hydration. On the other hand, there is a wide consensus that the issue of euthanasia does not arise in cases of palliative sedation, since studies have shown that high doses of opioids administered in patients at the end of life do not operate to shorten their lives. Consequently, the complexity of the aforementioned end-of-life decisions is intrinsically indicative of the presence of numerous ethical dilemmas that need to be addressed.

In this respect, questions surrounding medical decision-making at the end of life present particularly complex challenges, as they involve not only legal considerations but also ethical, cultural and religious dimensions. In the Malaysian context, these questions must further be understood against the development of palliative care services, the country's plural religious demography, the continuing significance of Islamic and other religious perspectives and the relevance of common law principles in shaping the medicolegal framework. Decisions concerning the continuation or withdrawal of life-sustaining treatment, the management of pain and suffering and the respective roles of patients, families and healthcare professionals often require the reconciliation of competing values, including the sanctity of life, patient autonomy and the professional responsibilities of medical practitioners. These tensions give rise to a number of ethical dilemmas that must be carefully examined in order to appreciate the broader context within which legal standards on end-of-life decisions operate. The following chapter therefore considers the principal ethical issues that arise in the decision-making process at the end of life before proceeding to examine the development of the legal principles in relation thereto.

References

Advance Care Planning Guidance Working Group, Ministry of Health Malaysia (2024) Advance care planning: A guide for healthcare practitioners in Malaysia. Ministry of Health Malaysia

Battin MP (2008) Terminal sedation: Pulling the sheet over our eyes. Hastings Center Report 38(5):27–30. https://doi.org/10.1353/hcr.0.0057

Berger AM, Portenoy RK, Weissman DE (eds) (1998) Principles and practice of supportive oncology. Lippincott-Raven
British Medical Association Ethics Department (2012) Euthanasia and physician assisted suicide. In: Medical ethics today: The BMA's handbook of ethics and law, 3rd edn. Wiley-Blackwell, pp 463–488
Cherny NI, Catane R, Kosmidis P, Holli K (2003) ESMO takes a stand on supportive and palliative care. Annals of Oncology 14(9):1335–1337. https://doi.org/10.1093/annonc/mdg379
Cherny NI, Radbruch L, the Board of the European Association for Palliative Care (2009) European Association for Palliative Care (EAPC) recommended framework for the use of sedation in palliative care. Palliative Medicine 23(7):581–593. https://doi.org/10.1177/0269216309107024
Chung I, Khoo S-Y, Low LL (2025) An insight into the experiences of Malaysian patients with advanced cancer and their preferences in end-of-life care: A qualitative study. American Journal of Hospice and Palliative Medicine 42(1):85–93. https://doi.org/10.1177/10499091241233599
Davis MP, Kuebler KK (2007) Palliative and end-of-life care perspectives. In: Kuebler KK, Heidrich DE, Esper P (eds) Palliative & end-of-life care: Clinical practice guidelines, 2nd edn. Saunders Elsevier, pp 19–32
Department of Statistics Malaysia (2025) Kawasanku. https://open.dosm.gov.my/dashboard/kawasanku. Accessed 20 Apr 2026
Garrard E, Wilkinson S (2005) Passive euthanasia. Journal of Medical Ethics 31(2):64–68. https://doi.org/10.1136/jme.2003.005777
Hamdan N, Yaacob LH, Idris NS, Abdul Majid MS (2023) Primary care physicians' knowledge and attitudes regarding palliative care in Northeast Malaysia. Healthcare 11(4):550. https://doi.org/10.3390/healthcare11040550
Harris J (1997) Euthanasia and the value of life. In: Keown J (ed) Euthanasia examined: Ethical, clinical and legal perspectives. Cambridge University Press, pp 6–22
Hui D (2014) Definition of supportive care: Does the semantic matter? Current Opinion in Oncology 26(4):372–379. https://doi.org/10.1097/CCO.0000000000000086
IMANA Ethics Committee (2005) Islamic medical ethics: The IMANA perspective. Journal of the Islamic Medical Association 37:33–42. https://doi.org/10.5915/37-1-5528
Islamic Organization for Medical Sciences (2005) Islamic code of medical and health ethics. In: World Health Organization Regional Office for the Eastern Mediterranean, Islamic code of medical and health ethics (EM/RC52/7). https://applications.emro.who.int/docs/em_rc52_7_en.pdf
Jabatan Mufti Negeri Selangor (2023) Pandangan hukum syarak isu-isu etika dan hukum berkaitan akhir hayat (end-of-life care). https://www.muftiselangor.gov.my/2023/10/27/pandangan-hukum-syarak-isu-isu-etika-dan-hukum-berkaitan-akhir-hayat-end-of-life-care/. Accessed 20 Apr 2026
Jawatankuasa Fatwa Negeri Perak (2018) Hukum eutanasia atau mercy killing. https://mufti.perak.gov.my/images/Fatwa%20tidak%20warta/2.HUKUM%20EUTANASIA%20ATAU%20MERCY%20KILLING%20%201.pdf. Accessed 20 Apr 2026
Keown J (2003) Medical murder by omission? The law and ethics of withholding and withdrawing treatment and tube feeding. Clinical Medicine 3(5):460–463. https://doi.org/10.7861/clinmedicine.3-5-460
Kinzbrunner BM (2005) Palliative care perspectives. In: Kuebler KK, Davis MP, Moore CD (eds) Palliative practices: An interdisciplinary approach. Elsevier Mosby, pp 3–28
Lattanzi-Licht M, Connor S (1995) Care of the dying: The hospice approach. In: Wass H, Neimeyer RA (eds) Dying: Facing the facts, 3rd edn. Taylor & Francis, pp 143–162
Lim RBL (2003) Palliative care in Malaysia: A decade of progress and going strong. Journal of Pain & Palliative Care Pharmacotherapy 17(3–4):77–85. https://doi.org/10.1080/J354v17n03_11
Lim ZN, Ng WJ, Lee CC (2023) Advance care planning in Malaysia. Zeitschrift für Evidenz, Fortbildung und Qualität im Gesundheitswesen 180:103–106. https://doi.org/10.1016/j.zefq.2023.05.019

Marker RL (2011) End-of-life decisions and double effect: How can this be wrong when it feels so right? National Catholic Bioethics Quarterly 11(1):99–119
Materstvedt LJ, Clark D, Ellershaw J et al (2003) Euthanasia and physician-assisted suicide: A view from an EAPC Ethics Task Force. Palliative Medicine 17(2):97–101. https://doi.org/10.1191/0269216303pm673oa
Medical Development Division, Ministry of Health Malaysia (1997) Palliative care services: operational policy. Ministry of Health Malaysia. http://www.moh.gov.my/images/gallery/Polisi/PALLIATIVE_CARE.pdf. Accessed 11 Dec 2024
Medical Development Division, Ministry of Health Malaysia (2010) Palliative care services operational policy. Ministry of Health Malaysia
Medical Services Unit, Medical Development Division, Ministry of Health Malaysia (2019) National palliative care policy and strategic plan 2019–2030. Ministry of Health Malaysia
Ministry of Health Malaysia (2023) Health white paper for Malaysia: Strengthening people's health, future-proofing the nation's health system. Ministry of Health Malaysia
Mohamad AH (2013) Comments on review of Civil Law Act 1956. http://www.tunabdulhamid.my/index.php/speech-papers-lectures/item/698-comments-on-review-of-civil-law-act-1956. Accessed 20 Apr 2026
Mohamad Ismail MF, Mohd Romzi NSI, Shahadan SZ (2024) Spiritual care in palliative contexts: Perspectives from Hindu family caregivers—A scoping review. Jurnal Al-Sirat 24(1):188–209. https://doi.org/10.64398/alsirat.v24i1.341
Mohamad Ismail MF, Sazali NFN, Shahadan SZ (2025) Faith and care: Insights from Christian family caregivers on spiritual support in palliative care. International Journal of Care Scholars 8(1):86–97. https://doi.org/10.31436/ijcs.v8i1.419
Morita T, Tsunoda J, Inoue S, Chihara S (1999) Do hospice clinicians sedate patients intending to hasten death? Journal of Palliative Care 15(3):20–23. https://doi.org/10.1177/082585979901500305
Multinational Association of Supportive Care in Cancer (2013) Strategic plan: Consensus on the core ideology for MASCC. http://www.mascc.org/strategic-plan. Accessed 20 Apr 2026
Nalliah S, Lim RBL, Rampal L (2021) Palliative care in Malaysia: The need to do much more. Medical Journal of Malaysia 76(3):279–283
National Institute for Clinical Excellence (2004) Improving supportive and palliative care for adults with cancer
National Quality Forum (2006) A national framework and preferred practices for palliative and hospice care quality: A consensus report
Quill TE (2006) Myths and misconceptions about palliative sedation. Virtual Mentor 8(9):577–581. https://doi.org/10.1001/virtualmentor.2006.8.9.ccas4-0609
Segarmurthy MV, Lim RB-L, Yeat CL et al (2024) Mapping palliative care availability and accessibility: A first step to eradicating access deserts in the low- and middle-income settings. Journal of Palliative Care 39(4):255–263. https://doi.org/10.1177/08258597231214485
Tallon C (2012) Ethics and end of life care. Journal of Observational Pain Medicine 1(1):1–7
Wong WJ, Hwong WY, Teoh CCO et al (2025) Stakeholder consensus of quality indicators for end-of-life cancer care in Malaysia: A modified Delphi study. BMC Palliative Care 24:311. https://doi.org/10.1186/s12904-025-01947-4
World Health Organization (2002) National cancer control programmes: Policies and managerial guidelines, 2nd edn
Wright M, Hamzah E, Phungrassami T, Bausa-Claudio A (2010) Hospice and palliative care in Southeast Asia: a review of developments and challenges in Malaysia, Thailand and the Philippines. Oxford University Press, Oxford
Yang SL, Woon YL, Teoh CCO et al (2020) Adult palliative care 2004–2030 population study: Estimates and projections in Malaysia. BMJ Supportive & Palliative Care 12(e1):e129–e136. https://doi.org/10.1136/bmjspcare-2020-002283

Chapter 2
Ethical Dimensions and Professional Ethical Guidance on End-of-Life Decisions

Abstract This chapter examines the principal ethical dimensions of end-of-life decisions and the manner in which biomedical principles guide difficult clinical choices. It begins by outlining the governing ethical principles of sanctity of life, beneficence, non-maleficence, autonomy and justice and then analyses the dilemmas that arise when these principles come into tension in practice. Particular attention is given to withholding and withdrawal of life-sustaining treatment, palliative and terminal sedation, medical futility, distributive justice and the distinction between "killing" and "letting die". The chapter shows that although respect for autonomy is central to contemporary bioethics, it is not absolute and must be assessed in relation to the patient's best interests, vulnerability, quality of life and the doctor's professional obligations. It further contends that end-of-life decisions should not be reduced to purely clinical judgement but should instead be approached through structured shared decision-making that accommodates communication, capacity assessment, family involvement and the patient's values and beliefs. The chapter also examines Malaysian professional ethical codes, clinical guidelines and palliative care standards insofar as they reflect and operationalise these ethical principles in local end-of-life care. In the Malaysian context, these instruments are significant in demonstrating that ethical end-of-life care must remain responsive to religion, culture, family involvement and local clinical realities.

2.1 Introduction

Since the turn of the twentieth century, the increase in the degree of medical prevalence particularly at the end of life has redefined the dimensions between life and death. Medical treatment and equipment are now able to prolong the life expectancy of patients suffering from life-limiting illnesses even in the absence of any brain activity. Resultantly, the emergence of sophisticated medical devices and treatment such as life-sustaining interventions has raised many ethical issues relating to death and dying, delicate subject matters where a patient's personal values are especially significant. Thus, decision-making in end-of-life care is often an intricate process,

F. Alias, P. N. Jahn Kassim, *Ethics and the Law on End-of-Life Decisions in Malaysia*, https://doi.org/10.1007/978-981-92-3625-1_2

as the clinical evaluation of a terminally ill patient not only involves his or her physiological prognosis but considerations relating to the patient's emotional and psychosocial well-being. In doing so, doctors must also accord respect to the patient's right of self-determination which now forms the paramount consideration in medical decision-making, taking precedence over medical paternalism, amidst the fears that one's dying phase would be suspended indefinitely by medical intervention. As a result, doctors are often confronted with the uneasy and complex task of striking a balance between their own set of moral values and their ethical responsibilities towards patients and the society at large while at the same time being duty-bound to honour a patient's personal choices. This chapter seeks to highlight the ethical dilemmas faced by doctors in end-of-life care and concomitantly examine the application and interplay of biomedical principles in end-of-life decisions, in order to facilitate a more cohesive understanding on how such ethical standards may assist in guiding the decision-making process.

2.2 Governing Ethical Principles in End-of-Life Decision-Making

Ethics is classified as a sub-branch of applied philosophy that is intrinsically related to morality. The correlation between ethics and morality is that morality refers to social norms that distinguish from right and wrong, while ethics describes moral conduct based on the character and principles in each profession. Medical ethics constitute a subdivision of ethics which is intrinsically linked to the application of clinical skills and knowledge. Medical ethics are essential in guiding medical judgements that need to be made for delivering what would be in the best interests of the patient. They provide the fundamentals for good decision-making and professional conduct for the medical profession and regulate the nature of relationship between doctor and patient. Accordingly, the moral dimension is a central component of medical practice as the primary function of medicine is not only "to cure illness...but to cure people of their illnesses".[1] Ethical standards not only promote the purpose of medical care, which is to relieve suffering, but also moral and social values, and provide a framework to facilitate a comfortable and therapeutic healthcare environment. It is therefore important to have a clear understanding of bioethical principles, particularly in dealing with end-of-life situations where personal values and beliefs may come into conflict. This will help healthcare personnel to properly apply them in identifying and evaluating ethical issues in end-of-life care and in recommending solutions for each particular clinical situation.

[1] Steinberg (2003), pp. 389–404.

2.2.1 Sanctity of Life

The sanctity of life is a fundamental and paramount axiom that transcends all religions, cultures and communities in the world. From time immemorial, mankind has inherently considered life to be precious and inviolable, which cannot be taken away even upon voluntary consent. The doctrine principally has its roots in the religious notion that life is a trust and gift from God, which must be respected, protected and preserved.

There is no one definitive definition of "sanctity of life". Nevertheless, traditional and modern ethics concur that it embodies the idea that life is sacrosanct and must be treated with the utmost respect and dignity. An intentional act to end one's life threatens the core of this doctrine and is considered to be a grievous wrong. According to the *Oxford English Dictionary*, "sanctity" in the present context is defined as "ultimate importance and inviolability". Kuhse states the sanctity-of-life ethics is one that "absolutely prohibits the termination of life and that sees all human life, regardless of its type or quality, as of infinite and intrinsic worth".[2] Some ethicists are of the opinion that the value of life is ultimately grounded in its sanctity and quality, which must be protected and allowed to flourish for the mutual good of the individual and society at large,[3] while others aver that the concept of inviolability lies beyond the value of physiological existence; rather, it relates to the moral attitude and actions undertaken by an individual in sanctifying his or her life.[4]

The inviolability principle is especially significant in the medical context because of its direct nexus with the ethical duty to prevent harm, i.e. non-maleficence. The Hippocratic Oath, which is one of the earliest and widely known codes of medical practice, contains the following sentence which acknowledges the sanctity of life: "I will give no deadly medicine to anyone if asked, nor suggest any such counsel; and in like manner I will not give to a woman a pessary to produce abortion". The first provision of the International Code of Medical Ethics which is based on the Declaration of Geneva (the modern restatement of the Hippocratic Oath) similarly states that "a doctor must always bear in mind the obligations of preserving human life".

It is to be noted that despite the fact that both the modern and theological concepts on the inviolability principle are quite similar, a marked difference exists; while modern ethics view sanctity on the basis of the intrinsic value of human life, several major religions in particular Islam, Judaism and Christianity attribute the sacredness of the principle to the fact that all life comes from and belongs to God and only God has the right to take it away. Human beings must therefore protect the gift of life to the best of their ability. To intentionally commit any act which threatens and violates its sanctity is to blatantly defy the will of God and place the wrongdoer in sin.

---

[2] Kuhse (1981), p. 75.

[3] See, for instance, Omoyefa (2010), pp. 99–105.

[4] See, for instance, Baranzke (2012), pp. 295–308.

Although the concept of sanctity is centred on the inviolability of human life, many ethicists have been reluctant to equate it with vitalism and have sought to distinguish between the two. Vitalism holds human life to be of an absolute supreme value which prevails over all other basic goods and must be preserved at all costs. On the other hand, sanctity of life carries a different connotation: while life has an inherent value in itself that renders it sacrosanct, it is not an absolute good to the exclusion of all other elements. It recognises death as a definite and natural end to the process of life, and thus, any measure undertaken to hasten or unnecessarily prolong life is considered to be unethical. Further, intention plays an important role in determining whether one's life has indeed been violated and that in situations such as just war and self-defence, the taking of life is deemed permissible. According to ethicists such as Pellegrino,[5] the doctrine of sanctity of life is by nature incongruent with vitalism, as the latter embodies the implausible concept of preserving life indeterminately, whereas the inviolability principle does not impose a moral obligation to maintain life by imposing life-sustaining measures that are excessive and costly and would not be in the patient's best interests. The sanctity of life therefore requires a balance to be drawn between the effectiveness that a certain measure would have in prolonging the life of an individual and its impact on his or her emotional, social and economic well-being. The assessment of such factors represents considerations of quality of life that influence end-of-life decisions.

2.2.2 *Beneficence*

The duty to do good and promote a patient's well-being, and not merely the avoidance of harm, is considered to be the primary aim and raison d'être of medicine. This is embodied in the Hippocratic Oath where doctors undertake to apply all necessary measures "for the benefit of the sick" according to their best abilities and judgement. Thus, when deciding between two options of therapy, doctors must choose that which would be capable of maximising the benefits to the patient. Beneficence entails that doctors place their patients' interests before their own, and this includes providing the patient with relevant and sufficient information, discussing the course of treatment that would most benefit the patient and finding out what the patient's wishes are. This duty however does not impose an unqualified duty on doctors to adhere to the patient's requests, and exceptions may occur in situations where the latter would not benefit or cause more harm to the patient itself or that such requests contravene the law and/or the doctor's professional code of ethics.

An example of a contraindicative situation where beneficence is applied are cases of medical futility. When a course of treatment is futile, the doctor's obligation to carry it out is negated due to the fact that it will not provide the intended benefit to the patient. Conversely, a beneficial treatment may need to be evaluated

[5] Pellegrino (2000), pp. 219–241.

against the socio-economic reality of allocating healthcare resources, which entails the need for a balanced interplay between the principles of beneficence and justice. One of the central conceptualisations in healthcare policies is that the distribution of resources should not be concentrated towards a certain group of patients but should be made available to realise the greater medical good for a wider segment of those on the receiving end of medical care. The duty of beneficence therefore cannot lead to unfair and unjust provision of healthcare resources, which is discussed further in the succeeding paragraphs.

2.2.3 Non-maleficence

The principle of non-maleficence is derived from the maxim *primum non nocere*, meaning "above all, do no harm", and forms one of the basic axioms in medical ethics. It asserts a duty upon doctors to not inflict harm on patients which also includes an obligation to not impose the latter to harmful risks. This does not however require the absolute absence of harm from any medical course of action, as the principle recognises that medical treatments may also contain undesirable side effects. Thus, non-maleficence is applied on the basis that the potential benefit of a therapy should outweigh its harmful effects.

This in turn relates to the significant bearing of the principle of non-maleficence in the doctrine of double effect, which is recognised as a legitimate approach to justify the ethicality and legality of a particular medical therapy. This doctrine is based upon the rule of proportionality and applicable in situations where the proposed action has both good and bad consequences. In order for such action to be morally permissible, the following four principles must be satisfied:

(i) The act is not in itself immoral or is at least morally neutral.
(ii) The act is undertaken for the purpose of achieving the good effect, and is not intended to bring about the bad outcome, although the bad outcome may be foreseeable.
(iii) The good outcome is not obtained by means of the possible bad outcome.
(iv) The action is carried out for a proportionately grave reason, i.e. the good outcome outweighs the bad outcome.

The application of non-maleficence works in tandem with other bioethical principles, creating a practical interaction in the discharge of a doctor's duties and obligations towards his patient. For instance, although it is incumbent upon doctors to respect a patient's decision under the rule of autonomy, the duty to do no harm counterbalances this requirement by making it unethical for doctors to administer treatments that are medically unsound and would not be beneficial to the patient. Likewise, an equilibrium exists between the principles of non-maleficence and beneficence; while the former imposes an obligation on doctors to refrain from inflicting harm, the wisdom in beneficence requires doctors to take the active action to prevent and remove harm and do that which would benefit the patient.

2.2.4 Autonomy/Self-Determination

Autonomy is synonymous with self-determination. The word comes from the Greek terms *autos* (the ability to decide by oneself) and *nomos* (governance or the law to which one complies). The crux of autonomy is, thus, self-rule. An individual must be capable of determining his own life in accordance with his values, goals and beliefs. In health, it means a special form of personal liberty, where individuals are free to choose and implement their own decisions, free from deceit, duress, constraint and coercion. Therefore, autonomy can only occur in the absence of external control or pressure. A patient has a right to autonomous decision-making and should not be overridden by the phrase "doctor knows best". This concept is propounded by Beauchamp and Childress, which has largely influenced scholarly analysis on the concept of autonomy in bioethics.[6] According to Beauchamp and Childress, apart from being voluntary and not subjected to any controlling influences or constraints from others, autonomous decisions are those which are made with substantial understanding upon being properly informed. There is therefore a duty on the part of the doctor to disclose medical information that is necessary for the patient to form an autonomous decision.

Up until the twentieth century, medical ethics had taken a thoroughly paternalistic position, emphasising on the patient's well-being above any of his dignitarian interest. In the context of "medical paternalism", the term refers to interference by the doctor with the patient's freedom of action which is justified on the grounds of the patient's best interest. This concept stems from the idea that the patient is not and cannot be qualified to comprehend the technicalities of his own medical condition and that the medical attendant will do it for him, acting in the capacity of a benevolent parent. This aspect of doctor-patient relationship dates back to the Hippocratic Oath, where a doctor undertakes to apply "dietetic measures for the benefit of the sick according to my ability and judgment… [and] keep them from harm and injustice". The same commitment is also echoed in the Declaration of Geneva in the avowal, "the health of my patient will be my first consideration".

However, the last century has seen greater focus being placed on patient autonomy with medical paternalism being pushed to the backseat. The modern approach that patients are to be adequately informed and play the central role in decisions regarding their own medical care forms "the most significant challenge of the bioethics movement to conventional medicine".[7] The move from paternalism to patient autonomy is clearly illustrated by comparing the 1847 and 1990 ethical codes of the American Medical Association ("AMA"). Section 6 of article II of the 1847 AMA ethical code entitled "Obligations of patients to their physicians" contains the following statement:

> The obedience of a patient to the prescriptions of his physician should be prompt and implicit. He should never permit his own crude opinions as to their fitness, to influence his

[6] Beauchamp and Childress (2001), pp. 58–60.

[7] Baumgarten (1999), p. 1.

> attention to them. A failure in one particular may render an otherwise judicious treatment dangerous, and even fatal.

The opinion issued by AMA in 1990 under "Fundamental Elements of the Patient-Physician Relationship", however, takes on a different standpoint on the matter. It reads:

> The patient has the right to make decisions regarding the health care that is recommended by his or her physician. Accordingly, patients may accept or refuse any recommended medical treatment.[8]

The strong deference to patient autonomy is attributable to several factors such as the emphasis on individualism and self-responsibility and rapid technological advancements. The emergence of sophisticated devices and treatment in medicine such as life-sustaining interventions, for example, prompted a lot of ethical issues pertaining to the dying process, where patients' values mattered the most. Further, the doctor-patient relationship began to take on a different dimension as patients gained easy access to medical information, resulting in decreased reliance on the doctor and the augmentation of medical awareness. The main argument against medical paternalism is that the doctor cannot and can never know enough about their patient's values, wants, needs, interests, hopes and fears in order to make decisions for them. For instance, before a patient is subjected to any treatment, patient autonomy requires that all the relevant information about his condition and possible modes of treatment coupled with their risks, benefit and side effects be made available to the patient. Medical paternalism, on the other hand, views that patients are generally incapable of understanding medical assessment of risks and benefit; as laymen, they lack medical training and the relevant experience, and thus, patients cannot possibly be entrusted to make sound medical judgements.

Autonomy is considered by many to be the most important bioethical principle in medical practice. It is the fundamental right of the patient to conduct and manage his own affairs, including deciding what should be done with his body. Therefore, under the principle of autonomy, a patient is entitled to choose medically sound treatments and refuse undesired interventions, which doctors are duty-bound to respect. Patients' preferences are to be given priority since medical decisions reflect value judgements, and patients are therefore the best authority to decide their own values and goals rather than doctors. The doctor-patient covenant is seriously breached if the doctor offers medical procedures that conflict with the patient's values. As respect for autonomy or the right to self-determination becomes an important precept in ethical medical conduct, the doctor "may not restrict nor negate the free wishes of an individual with respect to his own body…[o]ne must facilitate any desired action acceptable to a person's own judgment and in accordance with his own choice".[9] Accordingly, to infringe a patient's autonomy is "to deprive him of one essential component of his own good",[10] and this violates the aim of medicine to act for the good of the patient.

---

[8] This statement remains a fundamental principle under Opinion 1.1.3 of the current AMA Code of Medical Ethics.

[9] Steinberg (2003), p. 395.

[10] Pellegrino and Thomasma (1987), p. 36.

2.2.5 *Justice*

The principle of justice in the context of bioethics requires equity to be exercised in the allocation of healthcare resources and services. It necessitates fair adjudication in the delivery of healthcare at the individual level in ensuring that the patient receives fair treatment and at the societal level in terms of just distribution of healthcare resources. In practice, different healthcare policies may adopt distinct strategic measures to implement social justice; some employ the cost-benefit analysis, which measures both the benefits and economic costs, while others implement cost-effectiveness analysis, in which the assessment of benefits is based on life expectancy, quality-adjusted life years or type of illness. Although there may be no concordance on a particular single scheme, the common goal of healthcare policies is to promote a fair access to basic healthcare for each individual. Medical decisions in end-of-life care, however, are relatively more difficult since they involve the allocation of scarce life-sustaining treatments that cannot be provided to every patient.

The above form of rationing for patients at the end of life, which is referred to as "micro allocation", involves creating a just balance between several criteria: (1) the treatment's likelihood of success, so that scarce resources are distributed to patients who can reasonably benefit from it; (2) medical utility, which focuses on maximising a patient's welfare and needs; and (3) the avoidance of wastage and inappropriate utilisation of resources that can be applied towards treating and saving more people. Some ethicists aver that the rule of justice must also be applied in cases where a terminally ill and/or dying patient requests for certain medical therapies to be continued, by evaluating such a decision against the consequential benefits and costs.[11] Therefore, it is ethically acceptable for healthcare providers to deny the patient's demands if there is cogent evidence that the treatment requested carries little or no benefit or when inordinate public funds would be needed to provide such treatment, which would result in an inefficient use of resources. It is important to note, however, that doctors should not withhold or withdraw treatment solely on the basis of resource constraints but instead prudently balance their professional obligations in delivering a good standard of care towards patients, with their duties towards funding bodies and society at large.

2.3 Ethical Dilemmas in End-of-Life Decision-Making

The most pronounced ethical dilemma in end-of-life decisions unequivocally lies at the core of bioethics itself: the sanctity of life. Both traditional and modern ethics subscribe to and uphold the concept that life is sacrosanct and must be treated with the utmost respect and dignity. Nevertheless, due to the advances in both technology and medicine in the past century as well as the shift in doctor-patient relationship, this has led to patient autonomy taking precedence over "sanctity of life".

[11] See Meisel (2008), pp. 51–54.

The above development has triggered several ethical dilemmas, particularly when the patient's autonomous choice is contradictory to what the doctor perceives to be in the patient's best interests and is antithetical to the doctor's moral obligation and professional integrity. Many ethicists contend that doctors have a moral obligation that may outweigh their duty to respect a patient's wishes, particularly where end-of-life decisions are concerned.[12] A doctor's obligation to his patient extends beyond the prevention of harm and includes restoration and improvement of the quality of life. Accordingly, it would be unethical for a doctor to adhere to a patient's request to administer treatments that are harmful or would offer no therapeutic benefit to the patient. This conflict is particularly predominant in aspects of end-of-life care such as active euthanasia, withholding and withdrawal of medical interventions and pain management.

2.3.1 Upholding Autonomy and Self-Determination

An ethical dilemma exists when the patient's choices conflict with what the doctor perceives to be in the patient's best interests. Modern law and ethics have recognised that the doctrine of sanctity of life can be superseded by the need to respect autonomy in cases of withholding or withdrawal of life-prolonging treatment. Since decisions on withholding and withdrawal of medical interventions have profound consequences on a patient's overall well-being, it is axiomatic for the decision-making process to principally take into account and not exclude a patient's values and preferences. In *Airedale NHS Trust v Bland*,[13] the court emphasised that "it is established that the principle of self-determination requires that respect must be given to the wishes of the patient, so that, if an adult patient of sound mind refuses, however unreasonably, to consent to treatment or care by which his life would or might be prolonged, the doctors responsible for his care must give effect to his wishes, even though they do not consider it to be in his best interests to do so…To this extent, the principle of the sanctity of human life must yield to the principle of self-determination: and, for present purposes perhaps more important, the doctor's

---

[12] See, for instance, Brett and McCullough (2012), pp. 149–150, and Billings and Krakauer (2011), pp. 849–853.

[13] [1993] 1 All ER 821. The case concerned one Anthony Bland, a victim of the disaster at the Hillsborough Football Stadium who suffered irreversible damage to his cerebral cortex which rendered him to be in a persistent vegetative state. He was fed artificially and mechanically with a nasogastric tube and showed no cognitive response to his surroundings. All his natural bodily functions had to be operated with nursing intervention, requiring four to five hours of nursing attention by two nurses daily. After three and a half years of remaining in this condition, a court declaration was sought by Bland's attending doctor to cease further treatment, which involved extubation, i.e. withdrawal of artificial nutrition and hydration and withholding of antibiotic treatment in case of infection. The declaration was based on a clinical assessment by medical experts that there was absolutely no hope of recovery for Bland and, thus, any medical intervention would be futile and not in the best interests of the patient.

duty to act in the best interests of his patient must likewise be qualified".[14] Further, "the patient's right of choice is not limited to decisions which others might regard as sensible. It exists notwithstanding that the reasons for making the choice are rational, irrational, unknown or even non-existent".[15] Thus, a patient's personal preferences in deciding their own course of treatment override societal interests in promoting the preservation of life.

The principle of self-determination requires that the patient's wishes be respected to the extent that if a patient of sound mind refuses to consent to a medical treatment which would prolong his life, the doctor responsible for his care must abide by the former's wishes, regardless of the fact that such refusal is unwise. It is to be noted that in the case of an insensate patient like Bland who lacks the capacity to validly consent or refuse medical treatment, the lawfulness of such medical treatment depends upon whether it was in the best interests of the patient.[16] In *Ms B v An NHS Hospital Trust*,[17] the court accordingly upheld a patient's right of self-determination. In referring to the judgements delivered by the bench in *Bland* on the interface between the two conflicting principles of autonomy and preservation of life, it was accordingly ruled that the principle of "best interests" was not applicable in cases where the patient had the mental capacity to make relevant decisions about her medical treatment. Therefore, a doctor was under an obligation to respect the wishes of the patient, even if it was plain to all parties, including the patient, that death would ensue.

Understanding a patient's preferences, which are usually shaped by his or her values and beliefs, is the first step towards respecting patient autonomy at the end of life. However, while it is generally agreed that respect for patient autonomy must guide the decision-making process, many proponents of autonomy recognise that it does not stand as an absolute and unequivocal doctrine. Respect for autonomy does not entirely necessitate complete discretion at the hands of the patient. True autonomy is not achieved by allowing the patient to unilaterally direct his own course of medical care with total independence from any external influence, relegating the

[14] [1993] 1 All ER 821, at p. 866 per Lord Goff.

[15] Per Lord Donaldson in *Re T (an adult: medical treatment)* [1992] 2 FCR 861 at p. 865.

[16] Per Sir Thomas Bingham in *Airedale NHS Trust v Bland* [1993] 1 All ER 821 at p. 843.

[17] [2002] All ER (D) 362 (Mar). Here, the case involved a patient who was mentally competent and had repeatedly yet unsuccessfully requested for the withdrawal of medical therapy to which she was subjected. Mrs B suffered a *spinal cavernoma*, which necessitated neurological surgery to remove it. During the course of her hospitalisation and treatment, she executed a living will stating that if, at any point of time, she was incapable of giving instructions, she wanted treatment to be withdrawn if she was suffering from a life-threatening condition, permanent mental impairment or permanent unconsciousness. Unfortunately, as a result of the surgery, Mrs B became completely paralysed from the neck down and was treated with a ventilator to ease her respiratory problems. She eventually regained some movement in her head and was able to speak, pursuant to which she requested to her clinicians on several occasions to have the ventilator removed. The doctors were not prepared to do so as they considered it to not be in her best interests, i.e. it would inevitably lead to her death. Mrs B then filed for a declaration claiming that the hospital had been treating her unlawfully.

doctor to the role of a technical expert whose duty is to provide the relevant medical facts to the patient and no more. In fact, to do so would instead infringe the patient's autonomy and defeat the patient's interests, as the patient would be left to make medical decisions on his own without full understanding and proper deliberation of what the situation entails. If doctors, for the sake of honouring individual liberty, were to allow patients to freely decide without making informed choices, this could place unreasonable responsibility on patients and lead them to make unwise decisions. Further, patients could be left feeling abandoned rather than autonomous if their doctors refuse to do more than provide them with options and leave it entirely to the patients' discretion to choose. Consequently, complying with patients' demands for unnecessary interventions that thwart proper clinical reasoning may also debilitate the professional integrity of the medical profession, as it "results in a non-deliberative, rote practice style that undermines clinical excellence".[18] Patients may be limited in their ability to comprehend the complexities of clinical issues, and thus, they should not be allowed to be actively involved in the technical aspects of the decision-making process. An alternative perspective suggests that the fluctuating values and emotional states often experienced by terminally ill patients make it difficult to assume that their autonomy can be fully restored or consistently maintained. Consequently, since individual autonomy can be significantly compromised in seriously ill patients due to delirium and decreased cognitive functions, this may impair their decision-making capacity. Accordingly, in a variety of circumstances in medical practice, patient autonomy operates on a wide spectrum, "ranging from very high, where patients make all decisions, to very low, where they have minimal decision-making involvement".[19]

2.3.1.1 Withholding or Withdrawal of Treatment: Patients' Wishes v. Medical Procedures to Prolong Life

The decision whether to withhold or withdraw life-prolonging treatments is often a difficult issue commonly faced by doctors in the management of patients in end-of-life care. Medical interventions such as resuscitation, ventilation and the use of antibiotics in cases of infection may operate to save and prolong the life of a terminally ill patient. However, such treatments may run counter to the wishes of patients who may request that these be withdrawn or may refuse them altogether. For example, in cases where the condition of the patient necessitates respiratory therapy by way of mechanical ventilation, some patients and family members may regard it as a burdensome and aggressive treatment that impedes what they believe should be the natural process of dying. Some patients may view CPR as an undesirable death-delaying act, which is in conflict with their values and beliefs that one should not alter and interfere with the course of nature, and consequently, such patients or their

[18] Brett and McCullough (2012), p. 149.

[19] Agarwal and Murinson (2012), e0017.

family members may seek a do-not-resuscitate order from their doctor. In these circumstances, doctors are confronted with the ethical dilemma whether to adhere to the patient's and family members' wishes or whether to decide on what is the best course of action for the patient. If death is hastened as a consequence of withdrawal of treatment, would such a decision violate the doctor's moral obligation to prevent harm to the patient?

The polemic that arises whenever the subject of withholding and withdrawal of life-sustaining treatment is mentioned is due to the pervasive perception that it is equivalent to killing or murder, which goes against the fundamental and inalienable right of a human being to live. Active euthanasia, which includes assisted dying, is considered to be an active and deliberate act of killing, while the withholding or withdrawal of interventions is viewed as letting a person die, which amounts to an omission. Whether these two fall into the same or different categories of conduct is a matter of dispute among ethicists. While most scholars maintain that there is a clear and valid ethical distinction between "killing" and "letting die" that justifies the prohibition of euthanasia and permissibility of withholding or withdrawal of treatment, there are those who argue that the act of killing and letting die are moral equivalents and should therefore be subject to the same ethical treatment.

(a) ***Arguments supporting the distinction between "killing" and "letting die"***

The first contention is represented by the act-omission distinction. According to this theory, in certain contexts, failure to carry out an act is less immoral than if one were to perform a different act, even if it is foreseeable that in both instances there would be identical consequences; as pointed out by Glover, "it is worse to kill someone than to let them die".[20] Hence, acting to kill a patient, even for good reasons, may seem wrong, whereas omitting to act by withholding life-saving treatment may seem right in certain compelling circumstances.

McLachlan maintains that the distinction between killing and letting die is valid; he stresses that there is a significant moral difference between actively killing a person and failing to prevent a person from dying.[21] He argues that notwithstanding that they may both be morally wrong, they are both still "different moral wrongs"; one is a wrongful omission, and the other, a wrongful killing. The manner of conduct in both cases is consequentially different, and further, it is not always morally wrong to desist from carrying out an act that would stop a person from dying.

The act-omission doctrine is very much correlated to the distinction between intention and foresight and must necessarily include discussion on the principle of double effect. There is a clear distinction between withdrawing treatment intending thereby to kill the patient and doing so but merely foreseeing that the patient will die. In the former case, murder has been clearly committed because the whole purpose of the act of withdrawal is to bring about the death of the patient, and clearly, the death of the patient is the aim of the withdrawal. However, in the latter case, the

[20] Glover (1977), pp. 92–93.

[21] McLachlan (2008), pp. 637–638. See also Kinsella and Booth (2007), p. 388.

death of the patient is not intended but merely an unintended side effect of the withdrawal. For instance, if the aim of withdrawing and withholding treatment is to relieve the patient from burdensome treatment which serves no worthwhile purpose, a doctor may properly do so as further treatment will be futile and will not secure a significant therapeutic benefit to the patient. In such cases, the doctor does not intend the death of the patient but merely foresees that nontreatment may or will result in the patient's life ending sooner than it otherwise would have. Thus, the effect of actualising this aim is a good effect, and the bad effect, viz. the death of the patient, is merely a side effect of this good effect.

Intention is therefore paramount in considering the ethicality of active euthanasia and withholding or withdrawal of treatment. In the case of euthanasia, the doctor prescribes a dose of medication which would be fatal to the patient with the express motive of causing the patient's death; death is therefore the means of freeing the patient from his suffering. On the other hand, when a doctor withholds or withdraws life-sustaining therapy from a terminally ill patient, it is not done to end the life of the patient; the fact that such medical action might hasten the death of the patient, though foreseeable, is not the purpose why it is exercised. Ardelt stresses this point by way of the following description: in active euthanasia, the obvious intention is to end the person's life, and if the patient continues to live after the procedure, it would be considered unsuccessful.[22] Conversely, in the case of where an intervention is withheld or withdrawn, death is not the aim, and if the patient does not die after the intervention has been withdrawn, it will not be a failure.

It has been argued that because death is imminent in the case of terminally ill patients, it is the underlying disease from which the patient suffers that is the cause of death, and not the withdrawal of life-sustaining treatment. On this point, a distinction can be drawn between active euthanasia and the withholding or withdrawing of treatment in the same way one can distinguish between the existence of actual causes and the absence of preventive anti-causes. In other words, failure to delay the dying process is not equivalent to causing it.

(b) ***Arguments against the distinction between "killing" and "letting die"***

On the other side of the fence, critics argue that the difference drawn between an "act" and an "omission" distinction is untenable and obscure. According to them, a decision to not perform or withdraw from certain acts is nevertheless still a type of action. It is further argued that there should be no moral distinction between "killing" and "letting die" because the decision in both cases is subject to the same moral appraisal and is the result of a deliberate choice (whether it be in the form of an act or omission), of which one must be accountable for its consequences.

Another contention is that frequently exercised medical practices at the end of life such as do-not-resuscitate orders and terminal sedation are, in actual fact, a type of euthanasia in all but name. This flows from the argument that both "killing" and "letting die" involve the participation of a doctor and reflect the patient's intent to

[22] Ardelt (2003), p. 424.

die, and the discontinuance of life-sustaining treatments is therefore seen to facilitate such intention, similar to active euthanasia. In both instances, death is the outcome of the doctor's intentional conduct, which the doctor is fully aware of, and the decision that he makes is based on such knowledge. The doctor is seen to play a lesser role in the patient's death in the case of assisted dying compared to if he were to withdraw life-prolonging interventions on which the patient is highly dependent on. Therefore, withholding or withdrawal of treatment should be seen in the same light as active euthanasia.

It is important to note that most medical experts aver that it is permissible to withhold or withdraw life-sustaining treatment and allow the progression of the patient's natural death. However, any decision to withhold or withdraw treatment should be based upon the expectation that the patient can no longer benefit from that treatment, i.e. that it is medically futile and the doctor's intention when doing so must be to relieve the patient of the burdens associated with that treatment. The ethical soundness in withholding or withdrawal of treatment therefore lies in the prevention of harm to the patient, i.e. the principle of non-maleficence. It is also justifiable on the basis of respecting the patient's autonomous right, in cases when the patient has indicated that he or she does not wish to receive such treatment.

2.3.1.2 Palliative Sedation: An Inhibition of Autonomy?

Another ethical dilemma is that terminally ill patients who are given continuous deep sedation are put into a state of reduced awareness, which results in the loss of their ability to socially interact. This gives rise to the fear that there may be potential abuse of patients who are rendered unconscious during the process, in which right to autonomy is inhibited. Further, not only is their ability to effectively communicate and partake in any further decision-making process regarding their medical care hampered, but this also affects the emotional state of their loved ones. Patients may accordingly refuse to be given opioid analgesia or choose to limit the level of sedation in order to preserve clarity of mind and awareness as much as it may be reasonably possible in the final days of their lives. It is to be noted that proper procedures of palliative sedation require an analysis of not only the clinical benefits and existential burdens associated with such treatment but also its effect on the patient's psychosocial needs, including his or her values and beliefs. This involves a systematic assessment and balancing between the severity of pain and distress, level of consciousness and adverse side effects. It is therefore important for doctors to adhere to proper practice guidelines on pain management, which include necessary engagement with the patient and his or her family members to discuss and address their concerns prior to initiating and in the course of administering such medical treatment.

Consequently, the principle of double effect can be made applicable to such circumstances. Thus, in this situation, the loss of interaction would constitute the bad effect, which is to be weighed against the good effect, i.e. providing the patient with symptomatic relief, consequently justifying the decision to administer proper sedation. This would not only serve to allay any ethical concerns not only on the part of medical professionals involved in pain management and guide them to act responsibly but also help comfort patients and family members who may require an ethical justification to address their fears regarding the consequences and side effects of such treatment.

2.3.2 Predominance of the Doctrine of Sanctity of Life

The notion that life is sacred and no one has the right to take it away except God forms the most predominant principle in the field of bioethics. Human life is intrinsically sacred and constitutes an immeasurable value that must be protected. Thus, it is not for human beings to determine when life is no longer worth living and bring about one's death, as doing so would be a grievous wrong, and from a theological perspective, this would be considered as acting against the will of God. In essence, the doctrine of sanctity of life enunciates an absolute prohibition on intentional killing and allowing a person to die, and that decision to prolong a life must be based on considerations of quality of life.

2.3.2.1 Active Euthanasia: Ending Life Prematurely

Active euthanasia remains one of the most debated topics in the field of medicine. The ethical controversy surrounding the issue of active euthanasia stems from the fact that it is an antithesis to the classic dogma of sanctity of life. Ending a person's life pursuant to the person's request is therefore seen as a flagrant breach of the axiom. In the medical context, the inviolability principle is especially significant because of its direct nexus with the ethical obligations of doctors to undertake actions that will benefit their patients (beneficence) and prevent harm to the latter (non-maleficence). Euthanasia is also heavily criticised as it is considered to be a grievous violation of both professional and moral integrity to empower doctors to end a life when their duty is to heal.

Doctors may face an ethical dilemma in cases where terminally ill patients assert their autonomy by demanding that their lives be terminated to reduce their suffering or be allowed to die with decency and dignity. A person's right to free choice forms the main contention of the proponents of euthanasia, where it is argued that if one has the right to exercise control over his life, one should also be entitled to choose when, where and how he should die. A more secular approach is adopted in that the decision to die is considered to be a personal affair and is not subservient to the impact it has on public interests. Some ethicists are of the view that it is unethical for those who strongly believe in the sanctity of life to impose the same notion upon individuals who desire that their autonomous choice to end their lives prematurely be upheld.[23]

It has, however, been largely advocated that a patient's right to autonomy does not encompass complex situations such as assistance in dying. Accordingly, it is considered unethical for doctors to undermine their commitment to professional integrity, at the core of which stands their moral obligation to primarily protect the patients' best interests, by succumbing to a patient's request to die. Although the right of self-determination necessitates that competent patients be given their right to choose which treatments to consent to and refuse, it does not apply for the purpose of condoning demands for active euthanasia. Orentlicher points out that since a person's choice to end his life may not be a genuine expression of autonomy, this leads to the strong predilection to prohibit the act altogether.[24] Although the refusal to accede to the patient's wishes may be seen as an infraction to the patient's individual liberty, it is averred that terminating one's life is in fact antithetical to his right to wilful and free consent as it puts an end to the possibility of the patient's right to exercise autonomy. This is due to the fact that the decision to hasten death permanently pre-empts any possibility of the patient receiving other beneficial interests that may come his way, such as bequests and advances in palliative treatment.

2.3.3 *Balancing Between Sanctity of Life and Quality of Life*

Although the classic proposition has been that sanctity of life must remain objective as it operates on the basis that all human lives irrespective of value and capacity are equally inviolate, in practice, considerations on quality of life largely influence assessments made at the end of life, which have to a certain extent led to a diminution of the former's objectivity.

2.3.3.1 Withholding or Withdrawal of Treatment: Incompetent Patients

An end-of-life decision on whether to withhold or withdraw life-sustaining treatment would necessarily warrant a deliberation on the sanctity-of-life ethic, since such a decision might result in hastening the dying process. This is particularly relevant in the case of incompetent patients, i.e. those who have diminished capacity to exercise proper autonomy, for example, insensate patients, children who are very young and those suffering from mental retardation.

It is pertinent to note that a doctor's obligation to his patient extends beyond the prevention of harm and includes restoration and improvement of the quality of life.

[23] See, for instance, Dworkin (1993), pp. 213–217.

[24] Orentlicher (1998), pp. 850–851.

Quality of life constitutes an integral and necessary component in evaluating what would be in the best interests of the patient and providing as humane and comfortable an environment as possible particularly during the final stages of his or her life. The AMA considers it permissible to consider quality of life in decisions involving medical interventions and acknowledges it to be a valid factor in determining the patient's best interests. Quality of life is to be assessed on a case-to-case basis, as it is characterised by and contingent upon a patient's personal values, beliefs and social influences, apart from clinical findings such as the patient's physical, sensory, emotional and cognitive functions, his or her medical prognosis, loss of dignity arising from the present condition and proposed treatment and life expectancy, as well as the risks and side effects of carrying out the proposed treatment. In *Bland*'s case, for instance, the futility of the treatment in providing him any quality of life ethically justified its termination.[25]

2.3.4 *Justifying Considerations of Medical Futility and Distributive Justice*

When certain interventions are considered to be clinically futile and confer no benefit on the patient, there is no ethical obligation to administer or continue such treatment. There is accordingly no breach of duty on the part of the doctor if he decides to cease treatment, since realistically, its objective is not attainable. Doctors are not under an unqualified duty to prolong life at all costs; accordingly the duty to provide medical treatment "ceases when such treatment can serve no humane purpose".[26] Some experts contend that such non-beneficial interventions should not even be offered to the patient in the first place, as this would impede the patient's ability to rationale and exert proper autonomy.

A related issue that has gained increasing attention in recent literature is the need to reduce low-benefit and burdensome interventions near the end of life. This should not be understood as a form of rationing, but rather as part of the ethical duty to ensure that treatment remains proportionate to the patient's condition, goals and best interests. Some interventions, although clinically available, may no longer confer meaningful benefit to the patient and may instead aggravate suffering, prolong the dying process or impose unnecessary treatment burdens. In this respect, recent discussions on the de-implementation of low-value end-of-life care and the deprescribing of unnecessary medicines are relevant to the ethical analysis of medical futility and resource allocation.[27] The issue is not confined to major decisions such as ventilation, resuscitation or withdrawal of life support but also extends to everyday prescribing practices which may continue by default unless they are

[25] [1993] 1 All ER 821 per Lord Goff at p. 870.

[26] *Airedale NHS Trust v Bland* [1993] 1 All ER 821 per Lord Hoffman at p. 856.

[27] Kien et al. (2024) and Malhotra and Andres (2025).

periodically reviewed. This is particularly relevant in the Malaysian context, as recent local research on deprescribing among patients nearing the end of life illustrates that medication review is increasingly recognised as part of good palliative care, especially where the risks or burdens of medication outweigh their benefits or where simplifying treatment would better serve the patient's comfort and goals of care.[28]

2.3.4.1 Withholding or Withdrawal of Non-beneficial Treatment

The determination of what may constitute medical futility itself raises several ethical concerns. The fact that such a decision rests solely in the hands of the healthcare providers may lead to possibilities of the discretion being exercised arbitrarily. For instance, there is fear that medical treatment may be discontinued and deemed futile not only because it no longer benefits the patient but because it would be more cost-effective to do so, particularly in the case of the elderly, the uninsured and segments of the community who are at a financial disadvantage. This is related to the concern that limitation in healthcare resources, in terms of medical professionals and personnel, medicine, equipment and infrastructure, may be used as a reason to ration the application of valued resources and discriminate its distribution to certain groups of patients.

Those who advocate medical futility as a legitimate and viable justification for withholding or withdrawing life-sustaining therapy argue that it should not be perceived as sounding the death knell for terminally ill patients and denying them medical care. First and foremost, futility can be determined by balancing between both objective and subjective elements: (a) effectiveness of the therapy in treating the underlying pathology, which is measured based on the patient's medical prognosis, likelihood of recovery and physiological status; (b) the patient's assessment as to whether such therapy is beneficial and worthwhile, depending on his or her personal values and goals; and (c) the burden that such therapy would impose on the patient in terms of physical, psychological, economic and social implications. Whether a medical intervention is morally justified is therefore contingent upon a finding that all three components are favourable towards the patient's best interests. Second, a doctor who is bound to abide by the ethical obligations of beneficence and non-maleficence would never rule out or refuse to provide any treatment that would benefit his or her patient. A determination of futility does not in any way vitiate the doctor's continuous duty to palliate and provide symptomatic relief to the patient and ensure the patient's comfort as he or she nears the end of life.

With respect to the concerns raised in relation to the economic considerations that may be involved, it has been suggested that these may be addressed by the proper implementation of advance care planning and futility policies or guidelines. Advance care planning which entails the issuance of advance medical directives

[28] Chin et al. (2026).

helps to instruct patients as to their autonomous rights and provides them the option of choosing alternative care programmes such as hospice care over aggressive life-sustaining treatments. This will serve to facilitate the decision-making process, allowing doctors to assess their patients' needs and wishes while respecting the latter's preferences on how they wish to be cared for at the end of life, and consequently allow for more efficient apportionment of healthcare resources.

2.3.4.2 Terminal Sedation: A Case of Futility or Starving the Patient to Death?

The ethical dilemmas in relation to terminal sedation are more complex than palliative sedation, as it involves the withdrawal of artificial nutrition and hydration. This aspect of end-of-life care is considered controversial as it entails the removal of the provision of food and water, which is considered to be the most basic sustenance for human survival. The act of providing food and water carries with it a significant social meaning and symbolically is seen as a show of respect for the life and welfare of a fellow human being. As such, decisions on terminal sedation are among the most challenging and emotionally difficult issues in end-of-life care.

Opinions vary as to whether the supply of artificial nutrition and hydration should be continued at the end of life. Some consider it to be a humane supportive treatment that lessens the patient's suffering, while others aver that it is a non-beneficial and death-delaying intervention that does not provide any symptomatic relief. The foregoing of artificial nutrition and hydration may cause anguish to family members who may feel that their loved ones are dying from thirst and starvation.

The medical reality is that in some cases, other palliative measures apart from terminal sedation may not be able to palliate the severe and intractable pain and burden suffered by a critically ill patient at the end of life. Thus, terminal sedation is typically used as a last resort to provide comfort and relief to the patient throughout the dying process, when all other treatments have been ineffective. Further, the provision of artificial nutrition and hydration may instead cause considerable physiological distress to a dying patient whose bodily functions are deteriorating and can no longer tolerate the intake of such life-sustaining therapy. For example, the continuous supply of artificial nutrition and hydration may cause the patient to experience stomach and intestinal discomfort such as distension, oedema, polyuria and excessive bowel movements.

Another controversial ethical dilemma is that while palliative sedation does not shorten life, the hastening of death is certain in cases of terminal sedation. There is grave concern that once artificial nutrition and hydration are withdrawn from terminally ill patients who are heavily sedated, their life expectancy is shortened and death occurs in a span of several days, although it has been suggested that there is no consistent evidence that artificial nutrition and hydration prolongs the life of patients who are terminally ill or facing imminent death. Some ethicists regard terminal sedation as a "veiled" type of euthanasia and cannot be justified by the principle of double effect. The contention is that since the cessation of artificial nutrition and hydration would not serve any palliative purpose, causing the patient's death sooner than later is therefore the only intended and inevitable outcome. The patient dies due to starvation and dehydration rather than the underlying disease.

In practice, the decision-making process necessitates a deliberation between doctor and patient or the patient's family members to weigh the benefits and burdens and determine whether the patient should continue to receive artificial nutrition and hydration to prolong his or her life. It involves a consideration of factors that are personally significant to the patient, particularly the patient's values and goals that would influence how he or she would want to be cared for in the final days of his or her life. Some patients may refuse to be kept alive by life-prolonging therapy in what they perceive to be an undignified state of being. It has been argued that the decision whether to cease such treatment is ethically justifiable by the principle of proportionality, a similar consideration in the case of other medical interventions. Therefore, if the burden of receiving continuous artificial nutrition and hydration outweighs the benefit of prolonged life expectancy, the decision to cease such treatment may be legitimate. It has also been suggested that the ethical dilemma may be addressed by way of informed consent. Published guidelines have incorporated and highlighted the important need for doctors to assess and ensure that the patient is capable of comprehending the effects of his or her refusal to receive artificial nutrition and hydration. This includes the requirement that the doctor's intention to relieve the uncontrollable suffering suffered by the patient due to such therapy be properly documented. Doctors must carefully broach the subject matter with sensitivity in explaining and clarifying the nature, purpose and procedures associated with the administration of artificial nutrition and hydration, which include the potential benefits, risks and burdens of such therapy. If the patient decides to refuse artificial nutrition and hydration, doctors must then respect the patient's autonomous right to do so.

Artificial nutrition and hydration therapy therefore is to be managed like any other medical treatment, and the decision-making process is to be conducted separately from that concerning pain medication. In terms of medical practice, the AMA, for example, does not differentiate artificial nutrition and hydration from other life-sustaining treatments which may be withheld and withdrawn. In this respect, Malaysian health practitioners appear to adopt a similar approach to the issue. More recent local guidance now provides greater clarity on the matter. The Ministry of Health Malaysia's 2024 Advance Care Planning: A Guide for Healthcare Practitioners in Malaysia recognises that decisions concerning artificial hydration and nutrition at the end of life should not be approached on the basis of rigid assumptions but by carefully weighing the likely benefits and burdens of such therapy in light of the patient's condition, prognosis, values and goals of care. The guide further notes that in patients who are actively deteriorating and dying, artificial nutrition does not generally confer a clear survival advantage and may instead impose further discomfort and distress. Where the patient is in the last days to short weeks of life, difficulty with feeding may itself be part of the natural dying process, and nutritional interventions do not usually play a significant role. In such circumstances, the focus of care should instead be directed towards comfort measures, including good mouth care and the alleviation of thirst and other distressing symptoms. Accordingly, the continuation or cessation of artificial nutrition and hydration is increasingly treated in the Malaysian context as a clinical and ethical decision to be assessed on the basis of proportionality, best interests and the overall aim of allowing a natural and dignified dying process.

2.3.5 *Adhering to Duties of Beneficence and Non-maleficence*

It is universally agreed among the biomedical community that a doctor's autonomy and moral integrity must also be respected, and thus, it is justified for doctors to refuse to accede to a patient's decision that may expose the patient to unwarranted harm. Doctors may also have a religious consideration that conflicts with their duty to respect a patient's wishes, particularly where end-of-life decisions are concerned. Further, patients' preferences are not definitive unless a beneficial medical perspective is present. It must be noted that a doctor cannot be obliged to authorise treatments that are clinically unnecessary. Doctors are therefore not obliged to honour requests for interventions that confer no medical benefit to the patient or treatments that would expose the patient to more harm than good, as this would constitute a direct infringement of the values of the medical profession, particularly in upholding the principles of beneficence and non-maleficence.

2.3.5.1 Palliative Sedation: Sedating the Patient to Death or Sedating the Patient While He or She Dies?

The duty to provide symptomatic relief to patients and maximise their comfort is considered to be the most important aspect of medical care, especially at the end of life. The obligation to do so remains throughout the dying process, until death takes place. Palliative sedation is administered at the end of life as a last resort to provide relief from intractable suffering or when other medical treatments are no longer effective. The administering of analgesics such as opioids has the effect of sedating the patient, thus easing his or her suffering and distress, which is representative of the principle of beneficence and non-maleficence. However, pain management may give rise to the ethical concern on the theoretical risk of respiratory depression which may accelerate the death of the patient.

On the risk of exposing patients to a premature death, two major arguments have been put forward to justify and dispel this notion. Firstly, it has been argued that studies have proven that the fear that palliative sedation hastens the dying process is unwarranted and is a notion that should be dispelled. The second contention is based on the doctrine of double effect, which is grounded upon two propositions: the doctor's motivation is to ease suffering, and the treatment must be proportional to the illness.

(a) ***Refuting the claim that death constitutes a side effect of palliative sedation***

There has been a general reluctance on the part of doctors to administer high dosages of analgesics to terminally ill patients for fear that it would precipitate the death of the patient due to the physiological depression of the central nervous system. One of the dilemmas faced is the ethical and legal accountability of doctors in performing such a procedure, which some feel would be akin to practising voluntary euthanasia and, thus, constitute a violation of their duty of non-maleficence. To this, it has been argued that there is a marked demarcation between palliative sedation and acts of active euthanasia on several levels: (i) the purport of palliative sedation is to manage the patient's refractory symptoms, which is effectuated by way of sedation. In cases of active euthanasia, the intention is to end the patient's life, which would put an absolute stop to his or her suffering; (ii) the procedure in which such intent is achieved is dissimilar. In palliative sedation, an analgesic is administered ranging from mild to heavy sedation, depending on the condition of each patient, which must be regularly monitored and reviewed. On the other hand, active euthanasia necessitates the use of a lethal drug to cause the immediate death of the patient; and (iii) the criteria for the actualisation of palliative sedation and active euthanasia are each measured differently; palliative sedation achieves its objective when the patient's suffering is assuaged and his or her quality of life is optimised, whereas an act of active euthanasia is considered successful when death takes place.

A more substantive contention against the notion that palliative sedation might shorten the life of a patient is that studies have shown this to be misleading. Clinical research have accordingly demonstrated that pain medication administered at proportionate levels which are carefully monitored do not cause and may be able to augment the patient's survival rate and enhance his or her quality of life. There is a broad consensus among palliative experts that respiratory depression rarely occurs as a result of pain medication and that there is no conclusive data proving that opioids hasten death when administered proportionately. In practice, infused dosages of sedation are titrated to the lowest degree in which symptomatic relief is achieved, and the patient's comfort is restored. The level of sedation may be intermittently increased or reduced to palliate the patient's distress, which is to be assessed regularly from time to time. When executed in such a way, pain medication does not operate to hasten death. Consequently, based on the above justifications, doctors should not be reluctant to administer analgesics and risk providing inadequate care and pain relief to patients at the end of life.

(b) ***Application of the doctrine of double effect***

Although it has been suggested that the lack of evidence proving palliative sedation to be fatal dismisses the need to justify the administration of pain medication on ethical grounds, the doctrine of double effect remains a cogent and well-established ethical principle that can be invoked in cases where death is a foreseeable but undesirable effect, i.e. the threat of death being hastened as a result of medical intervention is real, which may be due to the patient's condition. In applying this doctrine to palliative sedation, it would be ethical for a doctor to ameliorate a patient's pain and distress (the good outcome) even though he foresees that it may shorten the patient's life (the bad outcome), provided that he does not intend the bad effect (i.e. does not deliberately aim or plan to bring about the death of the patient) and provided that the patient's demise is not the means by which pain relief is achieved.

Having examined the principal ethical dilemmas that arise in end-of-life decision-making, it is necessary to consider how these ethical principles are reflected in Malaysian professional ethical codes, standards and clinical guidance. The following discussion does not seek to treat these instruments as legislation, but to examine the extent to which they provide practical direction to healthcare practitioners in Malaysia.

2.4 Professional Ethical Guidance on End-of-Life Decisions

In Malaysia, a number of ethical codes, professional standards and clinical guidelines have been issued by the Malaysian Medical Council, the Malaysian Medical Association, the Ministry of Health and professional bodies involved in palliative and intensive care. Although these instruments do not amount to comprehensive legislation on end-of-life decisions, they are significant in illustrating the manner in which ethical principles are incorporated into professional duties, clinical standards and decision-making processes at the end of life.

2.4.1 Ethical Codes and Professional Standards

The three main ethical codes governing the conduct of medical practitioners, in particular doctors and nurses, in Malaysia are the Code of Medical Ethics, the Code of Professional Conduct and the Code of Professional Conduct for Nurses. Supplementary guidance as to the relationship between health providers and patients is ensconced in Good Medical Practice, while the Patient's Charter enunciates and focuses on a patient's rights and responsibilities.

2.4.1.1 Code of Medical Ethics

The Code of Medical Ethics ("CME") was first adopted in 2001 at the 41st Annual General Meeting of the Malaysian Medical Association. The CME lays down guidelines for the proper conduct of doctors practising in Malaysia and is divided into eight sections ranging from ethical rules relating to doctor-patient relationship, setting up practice and the role of the Association's Ethics Committee in promoting ethical conduct and resolving disputes. Under Section 1, "Good Medical Practice", the CME recognises the belief in God as the foremost tenet in Malaysia's guiding principles and acknowledges the diversity of the nation's population in terms of race, religion and culture.[29]

Appendix II to the CME, "Perspectives in Medical Ethics", reproduces the classical and modern oaths taken by doctors that have consistently over time emphasised the duty of doctors to treat life as sacred.[30] It sets out the oath to be taken by Muslim doctors, under which they must avow to hold human life as precious and sacred and to protect and honour it at all times and under all circumstances in accordance with Islamic law. Appendix II also sets out guidelines on the medical ethics to be observed by doctors of Indian and Chinese cultures.

Accordingly, the moral obligation to preserve the sanctity of life, which forms the most fundamental ethical dogma in theological and modern bioethics, is emphasised in Section 2.34 of the CME, where it is stated that the utmost respect for human life should be preserved and no medical knowledge contrary to the laws of humanity should be applied.

Two provisions in the CME are worthy of note in relation to patient autonomy and end-of-life decisions: Section 2.1 on "Consent of Medical Examination and Treatment" and Section 2.13 on "The Dying Patient". The guidelines on obtaining consent of the patient to medical treatment under Section 2 are summarised as follows:

(a) Doctors should provide information to patients in a manner they can easily comprehend and respecting the rights of patients to be fully involved in decisions about their care.[31]
(b) In the case of patients who are of the age of majority (18 years and above), consent should be provided of their own free will and without undue influence.[32]
(c) A doctor may treat a patient without his/her consent if the patient is incompetent provided that both the treating doctor and a second medical practitioner agree on such course of action.[33]

The issue of withholding and withdrawal of treatment is addressed in Section 2.13 of the CME, which contains some reference to the approach that doctors should adopt. Doctors should ensure that the dying process of the patient occurs with dignity and comfort "where death is deemed to be imminent and where curative or life-prolonging treatment appears to be futile". The section further provides that medical futility is a valid cause for discontinuance of treatment and recognises the need for doctors to consider any advance directive made by the patient and the wishes of his family members.

[29] Malaysian Medical Association (2023).

[30] Under the Hippocratic Oath, a doctor must make the following statement: "I will give no deadly medicine to anyone if asked, nor suggest any such counsel; and in like manner I will not give to a woman a pessary to produce abortion"; and in the International Code of Medical Ethics, which is based on the modern restatement of the Hippocratic Oath known as the Declaration of Geneva, the first duty of the doctor in treating patients is that he or she "must always bear in mind the obligations of preserving human life".

[31] Section 2.1.6 of the Code of Medical Ethics (2023).

[32] Section 2.1.7 of the Code of Medical Ethics (2023).

[33] Section 2.6 of the Code of Medical Ethics (2023).

Appendix I to the CME makes reference to numerous declarations and statements made by international bodies such as the World Medical Association (WMA), the World Psychiatry Association and the United Nations. The following declarations of the WMA are of particular significance in reflecting the Malaysian position on end-of-life decisions:

(a) *Declaration on Euthanasia*:[34] Euthanasia, the act of deliberately ending the life of a patient, even at the patient's own request or at the request of close relatives, is unethical. This does not prevent the doctor from respecting the desire of a patient to allow the natural process of death to follow its course in the terminal phase of sickness.
(b) *Statement on Physician-Assisted Suicide*:[35] Physician-assisted suicide, like euthanasia, is unethical and must be condemned by the medical profession. Where the assistance of the doctor is intentionally and deliberately directed at enabling an individual to end his or her own life, the doctor acts unethically. However, the right to decline medical treatment is a basic right of the patient, and the doctor does not act unethically even if respecting such a wish results in the death of the patient.
(c) *Declaration on Terminal Illness*:[36] The WMA recognises that doctors and patients are often faced with a complex set of decisions regarding medical interventions at the end of life and calls for more focus in developing palliative treatments and improving the ability of doctors to assess and address the medical and psychological components of symptoms in terminal illness. In view of the factors that significantly influence medical care of the terminally ill such as cultural attitudes and religious beliefs, and the cost and availability of palliative measures in different jurisdictions, the WMA considers the formulation of detailed guidelines to be made applicable universally to be both unpractical and unwise. However, several general core principles are set out by the WMA to assist doctors in the process of making end-of-life decisions. Among others, the WMA insists that it is the primary responsibility of doctors to assist the terminally ill patient "in maintaining an optimal quality of life through controlling symptoms and addressing psychosocial needs and to enable the patient to die with dignity and in comfort". The patient's right to autonomy must also be respected with regard to end-of-life decisions, including the right to refuse treatment and request palliative therapy that may relieve suffering, although it may have the additional effect of hastening death. No doctor should administer any non-beneficial treatment to the patient.

It is important to note that in its preface, the CME states that the code "is not, and cannot be, exhaustive". It encourages doctors to find middle ground "conducive to the fulfilment of the patient's best interests and towards responsible professional

[34] World Medical Association (2019).
[35] World Medical Association (2019).
[36] World Medical Association (2022).

performance". When juxtaposed, these statements in the CME illustrate the need for a guideline to direct the conduct of doctors in dealing with ethical conflicts, which are especially prevalent in end-of-life care. This also accords with Principle 7 of the WMA Venice Declaration on Terminal Illness, which calls for doctors and national medical associations to promote "the dissemination and sharing of information regarding pain management to ensure that all physicians involved in terminal care have access to best practice guidelines and the most current treatments and methods available".

2.4.1.2 Code of Professional Conduct

The Code of Professional Conduct ("CPCM") is a quasi-regulatory document that outlines the minimum standard of professional conduct expected of a registered medical practitioner in Malaysia. Under Section 3.1 of the CPCM, "[t]he utmost respect for human life should be maintained even under threat, and no use should be made of any medical knowledge contrary to the laws of humanity".[37] Violations of the sanctity of human life, such as torture or other forms of cruel, inhumane or degrading procedures, are considered to be a form of conduct that detracts from the reputation of the profession.

Of particular significance is Section 1.14 on "End of Life Professional Management", which expressly provides that a practitioner's primary responsibility is to take measures in the best interests of the patient and that any decision to prolong life through life support or other measures, or to terminate such support, must be made in the practitioner's best professional judgement, in consultation with colleagues and the next of kin. The same provision also states that a practitioner must not be involved in euthanasia or assist in suicide while recognising that the practitioner may be confronted with a living will or advance medical directive and must decide whether to comply with it in consultation with the patient's relatives and next of kin. This provision is particularly important because it brings end-of-life professional management within the express contemplation of the current disciplinary code itself, although the instrument remains, in substance, a professional and regulatory standard rather than a comprehensive statutory framework.

2.4.1.3 Code of Professional Conduct for Nurses

The Code of Professional Conduct for Nurses ("CPCN") acts as a guideline for nurses registered with the Malaysian Nursing Board in discharging their responsibilities. The preamble to the CPCN states the contribution of nurses towards the

[37] Malaysian Medical Council (2019a).

health and welfare of society "through the protection, promotion and restoration of health; the prevention of illness, and the alleviation of suffering in the care of individuals, families and communities".[38] In an end-of-life care setting, the significant role undertaken by nurses is more pronounced as they, more often than not, form the first and most regular point of contact with patients and are directly involved in tending to the patients' physical, emotional and social care.

Clause 1.1 highlights the form of respect that nurses should accord their patients, including the respect for autonomy. A nurse is to work co-operatively with patients and their families and should respect decisions about a patient's care and maintain informed consent in the provision of nursing care to all patients. If a patient refuses treatment, it is the duty of a nurse to continue to provide the necessary support. Clause 1.2 states that among the standards of care to be exercised by nurses is "to conscientiously assess the physical, psychosocial and spiritual needs of each patient" and provide "compassionate and competent nursing care to meet each patient's needs". Perhaps one of the most important responsibilities of a nurse, particularly in end-of-life care, is to act as an advocate for an incompetent patient. This is mentioned in Clause 1.4, where "[t]he nurse acts to promote and protect the interest of the patient when he is incapable of communicating his needs and protecting himself". In the event of any breach of the CPCN, the wrongdoer may be referred to the Nursing Board for disciplinary action.[39]

2.4.1.4 Good Medical Practice

Good Medical Practice ("GMP") is a set of guidelines issued by the Malaysian Medical Council, which sets out the standard of professional care expected of Malaysian medical practitioners. Although not intended to be exhaustive, the GMP provides recommendations to doctors on how to conduct their practice and approach the doctor-patient relationship in adherence to ethical philosophies. The manner in which a patient's right to autonomy is to be respected, for example, is explained in Clause 4.4: it reminds doctors to not assume that a patient gives "implied consent" to every medical procedure and that this "would not protect the doctor in the event of any litigation".[40] Informed consent is crucial and must clearly documented, including any objection or refusal by a patient to any particular treatment. The possibility of postsurgical complications must be discussed with the patient, although this is to be approached with caution and wisdom, i.e. not in a manner that would distress the patient. It also requires doctors to be conscious of the cost of healthcare

[38] Nursing Board Malaysia (1998).

[39] Clause 6 "Disciplinary Proceeding" of the CPCN states: "Should there be any written complaint on any nurse, a preliminary investigation will be conducted by the disciplinary committee of the respective organization and there may be referred to the Nursing Board Malaysia for further action".

[40] Malaysian Medical Council (2019b).

and to appreciate that health resources are costly, precious and finite. These features are particularly germane to end-of-life decision-making, where the practitioner is often required to balance respect for the patient's wishes, clinical benefit, communication with family members and the responsible use of limited medical resources.

2.4.1.5 Patient's Charter

The Patient's Charter takes the form of a memorandum of understanding between the Federation of Malaysian Consumers Associations, Malaysian Medical Association, Malaysian Pharmacists Society and Association of Private Hospitals Malaysia, evincing their commitment towards promoting and enhancing the high standard of professional and ethical conduct in the respective areas of healthcare, as well as to protect and educate patients of their rights. The Patient's Charter is to be treated as an educational document that embodies the CME and correspondingly integrates the autonomous rights of patients in medical care. This is evident from several provisions under one of the two main sections of the Patient's Charter, which are known as Patient's Right. Under the Charter, the Right to Choice of Care, Right to Information and Consent and Right to Participation and Representation, for instance, state that the patient is entitled to adequate information and consultation relating to his medical treatment and thereupon the right to consent or refuse prior to any procedure being carried out. This includes the patient's right to partake in medical decision-making.[41]

2.4.2 Clinical and Palliative Care Guidance on End-of-Life Care

In addition to broad stipulations of ethical conduct that are applicable to the medical community at large, several policies and guidelines which specifically deal with issues prevalent in end-of-life care have been issued by the Ministry of Health and organisations dedicated to the advancement of palliative care, in order to assist and provide proper direction to healthcare professionals in treating patients with life-limiting illnesses. The discussion below therefore considers the relevant guidelines as part of an emerging body of local guidance which increasingly recognises the importance of patient autonomy, best interests, shared decision-making, family engagement, palliative care and advance care planning.

[41] Federation of Malaysian Consumers Associations et al. (2023).

2.4.2.1 Handbook of Palliative Medicine in Malaysia

The Handbook of Palliative Medicine in Malaysia is the first publication dedicated to providing guidelines on an array of topics in the practice of palliative care in Malaysia. Authored by local palliative experts and intensivists under the auspices of the College of Physicians from the Academy of Medicine and the Malaysian Hospice Council in 2015,[42] the first edition of this handbook covers aspects ranging from management of physical symptoms, spiritual care and communication skills to end-of-life care and ethics. Under Section 2, recognition is given to the importance of religious beliefs and customary values which may influence the patient's concept of death and dying, including an overview of how death and the dying process are perceived according to the four major religious groups in Malaysia. The third section of the handbook in particular is dedicated to address end-of-life care and comprises guidance on prognostication, assessment and management of the patient's needs, as well as an outline of the decision-making process with regard to life-sustaining therapy. Chapter 13, for instance, sets out the characteristics of assessment in identifying whether the patient has entered the terminal phase and measures to be taken in managing the patient's needs at this stage. This includes protocols on artificial nutrition and hydration and providing sedation to provide symptomatic relief. Chapter 14 focuses on end-of-life care in intensive care units (ICUs) and prescribes the processes involved in managing end-of-life decisions such as withholding or withdrawal of life support therapy, particularly the withdrawal of mechanical ventilation. Recognising that admission to ICUs involves the utilisation of limited resources, the chapter provides guidelines for practitioners to assess whether a patient would benefit from life-sustaining treatment and the elements to be considered in holding end-of-life discussions, which includes the need to prepare, educate and engage the patient's family in the decision-making process, as well as being attentive to their relevant needs and values. The assimilation of fundamental ethical principles, i.e. autonomy, beneficence, non-maleficence and justice in the end-of-life decision-making process, is elucidated in the final chapter. It includes guidance on the ethical approach to cardiopulmonary resuscitation and explains the Malaysian position on active euthanasia and how it differs from withholding or withdrawal of life-prolonging therapy. In addition, Chapter 15 contains important notes on advance care planning and recommends this as a means towards enhancing the doctor-patient relationship, as well as the delivery of patient-centred and high-quality professional care.

A second edition of the handbook was published in 2023 under the auspices of the Malaysian Hospice and Palliative Care Council.[43] The significance of the second edition lies not merely in the updating of clinical material but in the clearer structuring of end-of-life care as an ethical, communicative and decision-making exercise. The inclusion of dedicated chapters on "Basic Principles of Bioethics in Decision

---

[42] Lim and Diana Katiman (2015).

[43] Katiman and Lim (2023).

Making"[44] and "Goals of Care Discussions and Advance Care Planning"[45] is especially noteworthy. It indicates that local palliative guidance now engages more directly with the ethical architecture of serious illness care, namely, autonomy, beneficence, non-maleficence and justice, as well as the practical need to conduct timely goals-of-care discussions before crises arise. The prominence now given to these themes suggests that local palliative practice has moved beyond symptom control alone and increasingly situates end-of-life care within a framework of person-centred planning, ethical reflection and prospective discussion with patients and families. This development is of considerable importance in Malaysia, where the legal framework remains incomplete and clinicians continue to depend heavily on professional guidance in navigating end-of-life decisions.

2.4.2.2 Consent for Treatment of Patients by Registered Medical Practitioners

The Consent for Treatment of Patients by Registered Medical Practitioners ("Consent Guideline") issued by the MMC reiterates the importance of the ethical principle of autonomy in the performance of healthcare services and goes further to provide a more detailed guide on the circumstances, procedure, prerequisite and conditions of procuring consent, with the aim of establishing good medical practice and promoting quality professional healthcare standards Malaysian Medical Council (2025). This involves, among others, the need for doctors who are planning to perform invasive procedures to establish personal contact with the patient prior to the intended course of action. The Consent Guideline recognises the practice of holding group consultations between the medical practitioners involved, such as the anaesthetists and surgeons, with that of the patient to discuss the proposed procedure. It is highly recommended that the doctor who will perform the procedure signs the consent form together with the patient during such discussion or, if that is not possible, that such doctor is obliged to directly obtain the patient's consent before the operation is to take place.

The Consent Guideline is particularly relevant to the ethical principle of autonomy, as it reiterates the importance of valid consent, adequate disclosure and the patient's right to refuse treatment. It also recognises that where a patient's capacity is impaired, the doctor should take steps to identify a surrogate decision-maker and, where necessary, make decisions in the patient's best interests. These provisions are significant in end-of-life care because they locate consent, capacity and surrogate involvement within a broader ethical framework of communication, professional judgement and patient-centred decision-making.

---

[44] See Lam (2023a).

[45] See Lam (2023b).

2.4.2.3 Clinical Practice Guidelines (CPG) on Withholding and Withdrawing of Life Support in Children

The Ministry of Health provides a CPG on withholding and withdrawing of life support in children.[46] The aim of the guideline is to assist paediatricians and intensivists in forming clinical decisions through evidence-based information and expert advice. It covers practical issues in decision-making, pre-withdrawal preparation, the withdrawal procedure and post-withdrawal process. The paediatric guidance is also relevant in illustrating how best interests, parental involvement, family communication and the dignity of the child operate in end-of-life decision-making. Read together with the more recent Handbook of Children's Palliative Care Malaysia, it shows that paediatric end-of-life care is increasingly approached as part of a holistic care pathway involving communication, symptom control, family support and bereavement care.

2.4.2.4 Advance Care Planning: A Guide for Healthcare Practitioners in Malaysia

The publication of the Advance Care Planning: A Guide for Healthcare Practitioners in Malaysia ("ACP Guide") by the Ministry of Health in 2024 marks an important local development in end-of-life decision-making. For the purposes of the present chapter, its significance lies not in its legal status or enforceability, which will be examined in Chap. 4, but in the manner in which it gives practical expression to the ethical principles discussed above. The ACP Guide presents advance care planning not as a single form but as an ongoing process of communication and shared decision-making through which a person's values, life goals and preferences for future care are explored, discussed, reviewed and, where appropriate, documented. It also assists in situating advance care planning within ethically accepted practices of palliative and end-of-life care, rather than as a means of authorising intentional life-ending acts. It therefore provides an important Malaysian reference point for understanding autonomy, family involvement, best interests and values-based care at the end of life.

2.5 The Importance and Need for Shared Decision-Making in End-of-Life Care

The foregoing discussion on the ethical dilemmas that arise in end-of-life decisions lends further support to the importance of a structured process of shared decision-making. Such an approach best preserves the patient's right to free consent while at

---

[46] Ministry of Health Malaysia and Academy of Medicine Malaysia (2005).

the same time allowing the doctor to honour his or her professional integrity and ethical obligations. In this model, the doctor does not merely furnish medical facts and leave the patient to decide in isolation. Rather, doctor and patient engage in a process of deliberation on prognosis, treatment options, burdens and benefits and the patient's own concerns, values and beliefs, so that the eventual decision reflects both sound clinical judgement and the patient's conception of what would amount to appropriate care at the end of life.[47] Shared decision-making is thus of particular importance in end-of-life care, where medical choices are rarely technical in nature alone but are closely connected to dignity, suffering, family relationships and the manner in which the final phase of life is to be lived.

The increasing emphasis on shared decision-making also requires a more nuanced understanding of autonomy. While autonomy continues to occupy a central place in modern bioethics, contemporary scholarship has shown that end-of-life decisions are frequently made within a relational setting and cannot always be understood through a purely individualistic lens. Serious illness, frailty, fear, emotional distress and diminished cognitive function may affect a patient's ability to receive, process and weigh information in isolation. For this reason, respect for autonomy should not be confined to noninterference but should also encompass the creation of supportive conditions that enable the patient to participate meaningfully in decision-making in accordance with his or her values and circumstances.[48] A relational conception of autonomy is especially pertinent in end-of-life care, where patients commonly consult family members and those closest to them before arriving at a decision.

This also explains why the process of shared decision-making does not exclude all forms of medical guidance. Although the era of unquestioned medical paternalism has passed, it does not follow that the doctor must adopt a passive role. The doctor may still recommend, advise and even seek to persuade, particularly where doing so would improve the quality of the patient's decision or protect the patient from clear and unnecessary harm, provided that such engagement does not override the wishes of a competent patient. A limited degree of guided paternalism or soft paternalism may therefore be ethically justified where decision-making capacity is impaired or temporarily compromised or where further support is needed to restore the patient's ability to decide with adequate understanding. In this sense, beneficence and non-maleficence do not stand in opposition to autonomy but may operate to facilitate its meaningful exercise.[49]

The Malaysian position lends further support to the importance of this approach. Local studies have shown that patient participation in decision-making is shaped by family relationships, cultural norms and religious considerations while still reflecting a clear desire among patients to be heard and involved in matters affecting their

[47] See Baik et al. (2019), pp. 76–88, and Huang (2025), pp. 131–137.

[48] See Gómez-Vírseda et al. (2020), p. 50, and Ministry of Health (2024).

[49] See Saleem (2026), pp. 21–26, and Ministry of Health (2024).

care.[50] This is particularly relevant in end-of-life care, where doctors may sometimes be inclined to discuss difficult decisions primarily with family members or caretakers. While family involvement is often necessary and valuable, such practice should not displace a competent patient from the decision-making process. It is therefore important for doctors to first assess whether the patient retains decision-making capacity and, if so, to engage the patient directly before resorting to surrogate discussions. Where the patient has previously made his or her preferences known through advance care planning or other prior discussions, those wishes should likewise be taken seriously in determining the appropriate course of care.

These considerations are now more clearly reflected in national guidance. The Ministry of Health Malaysia's ACP Guide expressly recognises that medical paternalism is no longer acceptable and identifies shared decision-making as the most ethical and acceptable practice. At the same time, the guide acknowledges that doctors remain duty-bound to preserve life, avoid harm and reduce suffering and that advance care planning discussions should assist rather than replace clinical judgement. Significantly, the guide also clarifies that preferences stated in an advance care plan are intended to inform decisions made in the patient's best interests when the patient is no longer able to decide personally.[51] This development is important in the Malaysian context because it supports a model of decision-making that is ethically balanced, clinically responsible and attentive to the patient's dignity, relationships and values.

It is also important to recognise that the ethical burdens in end-of-life care are not borne by patients and family members alone. Doctors who are repeatedly involved in the care of dying patients are required to engage with suffering, grief, uncertainty and conflict in a manner that may affect their own emotional and professional wellbeing. Recent Malaysian research on emergency, palliative care and geriatric medicine physicians illustrates that patient suffering may in turn give rise to physician suffering, particularly where doctors are required to confront distress, loss of control, diminished dignity and the limits of medical intervention at the end of life.[52] This reinforces the need for shared decision-making to be supported not only by patient-facing guidance but also by proper institutional structures, including communication training, multidisciplinary discussion and access to ethics support where difficult cases arise.

Consequently, information sharing, careful capacity assessment and coherent discussions between the patient, family members and healthcare professionals remain the most appropriate means of facilitating ethical end-of-life decision-making. Shared decision-making should therefore be regarded not as a dilution of medical responsibility but as the proper framework through which autonomy, beneficence and non-maleficence may be reconciled in practice. It provides the means for doctors to honour both the patient's right to self-determination and their own

[50] See Ambigapathy et al. (2016), pp. 1–7; Lee et al. (2022), pp. 89–92; and Tan (2018), pp. 87–92.

[51] Ministry of Health Malaysia (2024).

[52] Sinnathamby et al. (2026).

professional obligation to act in the patient's best interests, thereby promoting a more humane and ethically defensible process of care at the end of life.

2.6 Conclusion

Ethical principles help serve as a guide to direct doctors' actions in applying clinical skills to deliver what would be in the best interests of their patients and concurrently resolve issues arising in end-of-life care. In this respect, the preceding discussions illustrate that although autonomy is considered to be the central theme of contemporary bioethics, it is not an absolute concept and is subject to limitations. Thus, the principle is not to be exercised in exclusion, and neither should it prevail over all other values. It follows that the bioethical rules of autonomy, beneficence, non-maleficence and justice together with the doctrine of sanctity of life should be applied in congruence with one another, leading to a harmonious synergy of values within the spectrum of bioethics. No assertion should be made as to how each principle ranks in relation to one another, and there is a need to weigh all relevant factors in each particular circumstance.

Medical decision-making at the end of life should not be reduced to purely clinical judgement but should instead involve a concerted and carefully structured process between doctor and patient and, where appropriate, the patient's family members or surrogate decision-makers. Knowledge, understanding and effective communication are therefore key factors, as these assist healthcare personnel in discerning ethical justifications in end-of-life decisions, while at the same time identifying the patient's personal values, beliefs and attitude towards illness, pain, suffering and death. In this regard, shared decision-making assumes particular importance, as it enables the doctor to respect the patient's autonomy without abdicating professional responsibility and allows a proper balance to be struck between self-determination, beneficence and the prevention of harm. Such an approach is especially important in end-of-life care, where questions of capacity, vulnerability, family involvement and the burdens and benefits of treatment often arise in a particularly acute form.

The importance of adequate and effective communication between doctor and patient must not be underestimated. This is because it plays a crucial role in minimising misunderstanding and resolving conflict, as well as in promoting a mutual and collective approach to decision-making. Accordingly, the ethical dilemmas discussed in this chapter demonstrate that end-of-life decisions require not only sensitivity to abstract bioethical principles but also a relational and context-sensitive process of deliberation directed towards the patient's best interests. In order to facilitate the above, there is a need for clear and properly implemented regulatory standards on end-of-life decisions which give due consideration not only to ethical principles but also to the characteristics of religion, culture and locality. In this respect, legal intervention assumes importance in safeguarding the rights and interests of both doctor and patient and in ensuring that such measures are properly established and applied with sufficient clarity.

References

Agarwal AK, Murinson BB (2012) New dimensions in patient–physician interaction: values, autonomy, and medical information in the patient-centered clinical encounter. Rambam Maimonides Med J 3(3):e0017. https://doi.org/10.5041/RMMJ.10085

Ambigapathy R, Chia YC, Ng CJ (2016) Patient involvement in decision-making: A cross-sectional study in a Malaysian primary care clinic. BMJ Open 6(1):e010063. https://doi.org/10.1136/bmjopen-2015-010063

Ardelt M (2003) Physician-assisted death. In: Bryant CD (ed) Handbook of death and dying, vol 1. Sage, pp 424–434

Baik D, Cho H, Masterson Creber RM (2019) Examining interventions designed to support shared decision making and subsequent patient outcomes in palliative care: A systematic review of the literature. Am J Hosp Palliat Med 36(1):76–88. https://doi.org/10.1177/1049909118783688

Baranzke H (2012) "Sanctity-of-life"—A bioethical principle for a right to life? Ethical Theory Moral Pract 15(3):295–308

Baumgarten E (1999) The concept of patient autonomy. Medical Updates 2(3):1–6

Beauchamp TL, Childress JF (2001) Principles of biomedical ethics, 5th edn. Oxford University Press

Billings JA, Krakauer EL (2011) On patient autonomy and physician responsibility in end-of-life care. Arch Intern Med 171(9):849–853

Brett AS, McCullough LB (2012) Addressing requests by patients for nonbeneficial interventions. JAMA 307(2):149–150. https://doi.org/10.1001/jama.2011.1999

Chin AAH, Lai PSM, McCarthy SA (2026) Deprescribing for patients nearing end of life: Views, barriers and facilitators of palliative care patients, carers and nurses. Support Care Cancer 34:303. https://doi.org/10.1007/s00520-026-10522-3

Dworkin R (1993) Life's dominion: An argument about abortion and euthanasia. HarperCollins

Federation of Malaysian Consumers Associations, Malaysian Medical Association, Malaysian Pharmacists Society, Association of Private Hospitals Malaysia (2023) Patient's charter

Glover J (1977) Causing death and saving lives. Penguin Books

Gómez-Vírseda C, de Maeseneer Y, Gastmans C (2020) Relational autonomy in end-of-life care ethics: A contextualized approach to real-life complexities. BMC Med Ethics 21:50. https://doi.org/10.1186/s12910-020-00495-1

Huang H-L (2025) Shared decision-making with palliative care specialist. J Hospice Palliat Care 28(4):131–137. https://doi.org/10.14475/jhpc.2025.28.4.131

Katiman D, Lim RBL (eds) (2023) Handbook of palliative medicine in Malaysia, 2nd edn. Malaysian Hospice and Palliative Care Council

Kien C, Daxenbichler J, Titscher V et al (2024) Effectiveness of de-implementation of low-value healthcare practices: An overview of systematic reviews. Implement Sci 19:56. https://doi.org/10.1186/s13012-024-01384-6

Kinsella J, Booth MG (2007) Ethical framework for end of life decisions in intensive care in the UK. J Natl Inst Public Health 56(4):387–392

Kuhse H (1981) Debate: Extraordinary means and the sanctity of life. J Med Ethics 7(2):74–82. https://doi.org/10.1136/jme.7.2.74

Lam CL (2023a) Basic principles of bioethics in decision making. In: Katiman D, Lim RBL (eds) Handbook of palliative medicine in Malaysia, 2nd edn. Malaysian Hospice and Palliative Care Council, pp 131–134

Lam CL (2023b) Goals of care discussions and advance care planning. In: Katiman D, Lim RBL (eds) Handbook of palliative medicine in Malaysia, 2nd edn. Malaysian Hospice and Palliative Care Council, pp 135–138

Lee YK, Ng CJ, Lee PY, Tong WT, Sa'at H (2022) Shared decision-making in Malaysia: Legislation, patient involvement, implementation and the impact of COVID-19. Z Evid Fortbild Qual Gesundhwes 171:89–92. https://doi.org/10.1016/j.zefq.2022.04.020

Lim RBL, Katiman D (eds) (2015) Handbook of palliative medicine in Malaysia. Malaysian Hospice Council

Malhotra C, Andres EB (2025) Breaking with the status quo in end-of-life care through de-implementation. J Intern Med 298(2):97–106. https://doi.org/10.1111/joim.20086

McLachlan HV (2008) The ethics of killing and letting die: Active and passive euthanasia. J Med Ethics 34(8):636–638. https://doi.org/10.1136/jme.2007.023382

Malaysian Medical Council (2019a) Code of professional conduct. https://mmc.gov.my/wp--content/uploads/2022/04/Code-of-Professional-Conduct-2019.pdf. Accessed 26 Apr 2026

Malaysian Medical Council (2019b) Good medical practice. https://mmc.gov.my/wp-content/uploads/2022/04/Good-Medical-Practice-2019.pdf. Accessed 26 Apr 2026

Malaysian Medical Council (2025) Consent for treatment of patients by registered medical practitioners. https://mmc.gov.my/wp-content/uploads/2025/09/Consent-for-Treatment-of-Patients-by-Registered-Medical-Practitioners.pdf. Accessed 26 Apr 2026

Malaysian Medical Association (2023) Code of medical ethics. https://www.mma.org.my/images/pdfs/Link-CodeOfEthics/MMA_ethicscode.pdf. Accessed 26 Apr 2026

Ministry of Health Malaysia (2024) Advance care planning: A guide for healthcare practitioners in Malaysia. Medical Development Division, Ministry of Health Malaysia

Ministry of Health Malaysia, Academy of Medicine Malaysia (2005) Clinical practice guidelines on withholding and withdrawing of life support in children. Ministry of Health Malaysia

Meisel A (2008) End-of-life care. In: Crowley M (ed) From birth to death and bench to clinic: The Hastings Center bioethics briefing book for journalists, policymakers, and campaigns. The Hastings Center, pp 51–54

Nursing Board Malaysia (1998) Code of professional conduct for nurses registered with the Nursing Board Malaysia, 1st edn. Ministry of Health Malaysia. https://hq.moh.gov.my/nursing/wp-content/uploads/2015/04/nursing_board_malaysia-code_of_professional_conduct_1998.pdf. Accessed 26 Apr 2026

Omoyefa PS (2010) Physicians and sanctity of life: Emerging ethical issues. Stud Ethno-Med 4(2):99–105

Orentlicher D (1998) The alleged distinction between euthanasia and the withdrawal of life-sustaining treatment: Conceptually incoherent and impossible to maintain. Univ Ill Law Rev 1998(3):837–859

Pellegrino ED (2000) Decision at the end of life: The use and abuse of the concept of futility. In: Vial Correa JdeD, Sgreccia E (eds) The dignity of the dying person: Proceedings of the fifth assembly of the Pontifical Academy for Life. Libreria Editrice Vaticana, pp 219–241

Pellegrino ED, Thomasma DC (1987) The conflict between autonomy and beneficence in medical ethics: Proposal for a resolution. J Contemp Health Law Policy 3:23–46

Saleem S (2026) Argument for consensual paternalism in shared decision-making: Rediscovering autonomy in Western bioethics. Bioethics 40(1):21–26. https://doi.org/10.1111/bioe.70003

Sinnathamby A, Ong YT, Lim SX et al (2026) Concepts of suffering at the end of life amongst emergency, palliative care and geriatric medicine physicians in Malaysia. Am J Hosp Palliat Med 43(1):85–93. https://doi.org/10.1177/10499091251317725

Steinberg A (2003) Ethics, secular. In: Encyclopedia of Jewish medical ethics: A compilation of Jewish law on all topics of medical interest, vol 2. Feldheim Publishers, pp 389–404

Tan MKM (2018) Considerations for introducing legislation on advance decisions in Malaysia. Asian Bioeth Rev 10(1):87–92. https://doi.org/10.1007/s41649-018-0048-x

World Medical Association (2019) WMA Declaration on Euthanasia and Physician-Assisted Suicide. https://www.wma.net/policies-post/declaration-on-euthanasia-and-physician-assisted-suicide/.Accessed 26 Apr 2026
World Medical Association (2022) WMA Declaration of Venice on End of Life Medical Care. https://www.wma.net/policies-post/wma-declaration-of-venice/. Accessed 26 Apr 2026

Chapter 3
The Relevance of Common Law Principles: Addressing the Lacuna

Abstract This chapter examines the relevance of common law principles in addressing the lacuna in Malaysian law on end-of-life decisions. Building on the ethical discussion in the preceding chapter, it considers how courts in the UK and Australia have given legal form to difficult questions concerning autonomy, sanctity of life, medical futility, best interests and the protection of vulnerable patients. The chapter begins by analysing active euthanasia and assisted suicide, highlighting the continued common law distinction between respecting a competent patient's refusal of treatment and intentionally assisting death. It then considers the legal justifications for withholding and withdrawal of life-sustaining treatment, including the act-omission distinction, the assessment of best interests and the doctrine of double effect. The discussion further examines the role of professional guidance, statutory developments and culturally sensitive care pathways in translating these principles into clinical practice. It concludes that the UK and Australian experiences are not to be applied without qualification but provide useful points of reference for Malaysia, where judicial authority remains limited and clearer legal standards are still needed to support ethical and lawful end-of-life decision-making.

3.1 Introduction

It is established practice that when issues of medical treatment are brought before the courts for resolution, the inherent ethical position that underlies such course of action ordinarily forms the first line of judicial discussion. The court will accordingly examine the ethicality of a medical decision before proceeding to decide its lawfulness from a legal point of view. Thus, in this respect, judicial treatment provides substance and legal validation to the operation of ethical principles in medical practice. The development and construction of a proper and comprehensive regulatory framework on end-of-life decisions, however, not only requires the intervention of the court but also the involvement of legislators and policymakers. This chapter examines common law principles on end-of-life decisions not as external models to be adopted without qualification but as sources of legal reasoning that may assist in

F. Alias, P. N. Jahn Kassim, *Ethics and the Law on End-of-Life Decisions in Malaysia*, https://doi.org/10.1007/978-981-92-3625-1_3

clarifying unresolved questions within Malaysian law. Malaysia does not yet have a specific statutory framework governing withholding and withdrawal of life-sustaining treatment, advance medical decisions, surrogate decision-making or palliative measures that may foreseeably hasten death. In this context, the common law experience of jurisdictions such as the UK and Australia is relevant because it has developed principles on consent, refusal of treatment, best interests, medical futility, acts and omissions and the doctrine of double effect. These principles are considered in this chapter for the limited purpose of assessing the guidance they may offer to Malaysia, bearing in mind the need for any legal development to remain attentive to local statutory provisions, professional practice, religious values, family involvement and healthcare realities.

3.2 Importance of Judicial Intervention in End-of-Life Decisions

Judicial intervention in the area of medicine has often been regarded to be pivotal, particularly in offering clear guidance in issues that raise ethical, philosophical and religious dilemmas. It has been advocated that the law functions as a means of controlling the ethical conduct of the medical profession in the interests of society as a whole, as evident in the remark made by Lord Hoffman in his judgement in *Airedale NHS Trust v Bland*[1] that "…medical ethics [is] to be formed by the law rather than the reverse".[2]

The fact that end-of-life care deals with sensitive and emotionally charged issues such as pain, suffering and the dying process often causes the doctor-patient relationship to be strained, which may result in a breakdown in communication. This might accordingly be more pronounced in circumstances where there are competing values between the doctor and the family members of an incompetent patient. Such conflict indisputably requires the intervention of an independent and authoritative "third party", a role that is best fulfilled by the courts, where a fair process of decision-making is ensured.

Consequently, there exists a strong tradition where courts have provided direction to healthcare professionals and clarified issues relating to the ethicality and lawfulness of their actions. A significant example is where judicial decisions have elucidated that the inviolability doctrine can be superseded by the need to respect the patient's autonomous choices. In *Chatterson v Gerson*,[3] the court held that right of a patient to decide for himself was a basic and inherent human right protected by common law. In terms of medical care, this encompassed the right of a patient to consent to or refuse treatment, and therefore medical treatment carried out without

[1] [1993] 1 All ER 821.

[2] [1993] 1 All ER 821, p. 858.

[3] [1981] QB 432.

the consent of an adult of sound mind would amount to unlawful touching or battery. A patient was entitled to choose whether to accept the treatment offered to him, and doctors would need to comply with his wishes, even though in their opinion such decision would be contrary to his best interests or reasons behind it were irrational and unjustified. This is now an established common law principle that provides assurance to doctors that it would not be unethical of them to concede to a patient's wishes, for example, to have life-sustaining treatment withdrawn.

Another justification for judicial intervention in end-of-life decisions is that the subject matter is one that substantially impacts upon social policy and welfare. Accordingly, the court constitutes an influential platform where such issues can be judiciously highlighted, leading to more extensive deliberations. This can be seen, for example, in cases concerning assisted dying, for instance, *R (on the application of Nicklinson and another) v Ministry of Justice R (on the application of AM) v Director of Public Prosecutions*,[4] which have reopened the debate on whether such an act should be legalised. Such high-profile cases often pave the way for more resolute measures to be undertaken by relevant regulatory bodies in order to review and address the issue, and therefore in this respect, judicial decisions represent a catalyst and effective mechanism for necessary engagement.

The relevance of this discussion to Malaysia lies in the fact that local judicial authority on end-of-life decision-making remains limited. In the absence of a substantial body of Malaysian case law on withholding and withdrawal of life-sustaining treatment, advance medical decisions and palliative measures that may foreseeably hasten death, common law decisions from other jurisdictions remain instructive. They do not determine the Malaysian position, but they provide a structured body of reasoning through which the legal implications of ethical principles such as autonomy, sanctity of life, best interests and medical futility may be better understood.

3.3 Developing Legal Standards in End-of-Life Decisions

In as much as the judicial involvement in resolving medical issues is accepted to be established practice, such intervention in itself may cause problems particularly when the courts find themselves drawn in to act as mediators in complex and frequently distressing clinical matters. Further, the judicial process may prove to be tedious and time-consuming, which may be undesirable where there is an urgent need for the matter to be resolved. In end-of-life decisions, where issues of public policy are engaged, courts are often reluctant to issue a declaration and will refer such matter to legislature for its further consideration. The succeeding discussions will accordingly demonstrate the judicial and legislative approaches with respect to the legal standards and issues of legalisation surrounding end-of-life decisions and

[4] [2014] UKSC 38.

assess the extent to which these principles may assist in addressing the current gaps in the Malaysian position.

3.3.1 Active Euthanasia and Assisted Dying

The legal justifications on issues relating to active euthanasia hinge upon similar ethical considerations that are preponderant in the debate on whether a dying patient should be given the right to end his own life, either by his own hand or with the assistance of a medical practitioner. Although the doctrine of sanctity of life, more often than not, lies at the heart of every medical decision-making process, recent legislative developments in some jurisdictions have brought renewed attention to the extent to which patient autonomy may justify end-of-life choices. Within the common law, however, courts have generally approached this issue with caution, particularly where the decision involves the intentional ending of life.

In Malaysia, the relevance of this discussion is not directed towards advocating the legalisation of active euthanasia or assisted dying. Rather, it is important because the legal treatment of these practices helps clarify the boundary between intentional life-ending acts and other end-of-life decisions, particularly withholding and withdrawal of non-beneficial treatment and palliative measures intended to relieve suffering. This distinction is necessary in order to avoid conflating lawful or ethically accepted end-of-life care with acts that are directed at causing death.

Although active euthanasia and assisted dying have been legalised or decriminalised in a limited number of jurisdictions, including the Netherlands, Belgium, Luxembourg, Canada, Spain, several states in the USA and, more recently, a number of Australian jurisdictions, such developments have generally taken place through express statutory intervention rather than judicial implication. This is significant because the legalisation of intentional life-ending acts engages questions of criminal liability, public policy, protection of vulnerable persons and the proper limits of medical practice. For the purposes of the present chapter, these developments are relevant only as brief contextual background. The focus of the discussion remains on the common law approach to active euthanasia and assisted dying and the extent to which its reasoning may assist in clarifying the Malaysian position.

3.3.1.1 The Legal Quandary Between Taking Away Life and the Right to Die

In common law jurisdictions, the courts have consistently emphasised euthanasia to be unlawful, on the ground that the intentional act of causing death is a gross violation of the fundamental principle that holds all human life sacrosanct. The law in the UK, for instance, does not recognise a separate category of "mercy killing" committed on compassionate terms and/or with the consent of the victim; and neither does it accept the defence that the act of intentionally ending the life of the victim was committed "in the best interests of the victim" as a valid justification.[5] A doctor committing an act of euthanasia would therefore be liable, under English law, for murder, unless the circumstances are such as to reduce liability to manslaughter. In terms of sentencing, however, while murder remains punishable by a mandatory life sentence, the element of "mercy" may be taken into account as a mitigating factor in determining the minimum term, as indicated in paragraph 10(f) of Schedule 21 to the Sentencing Act 2020. For Malaysia, this line of reasoning is significant because it maintains a firm distinction between respecting a patient's refusal of treatment and authorising another person to intentionally bring about the patient's death. The former is grounded in autonomy and bodily integrity, while the latter engages the criminal law's protection of life and the public interest in protecting vulnerable persons. This distinction is particularly important in a jurisdiction where end-of-life decisions are still not governed by a dedicated legislative framework.

In 2006, the UK set up a Law Commission for the purpose of reviewing the law of murder and manslaughter. A section of the report prepared by the Law Commission was dedicated to address the areas of euthanasia and assisted suicide, but only in so far as they related to the grounds for reducing it to a less serious act of homicide.[6] The Law Commission however declined to consider and recommend that "mercy killing" be categorised as a separate offence or as a partial defence, as it necessitated extensive consultation on important and complex issues that were similarly raised in the debate as to whether euthanasia should be legalised, which were beyond the terms of reference of their review. In light of the matter, it was proposed that the English government undertake a public consultation on the viability of amending the existing law to recognise "mercy killing" as an offence or partial defence and to what extent such modifications should accordingly be made.

In terms of assisted dying, however, the increased focus on greater patient autonomy in the field of medicine and the consequent judicial recognition that this prevails over the sanctity of life since the past century have led to important shifts under the common law. The difference in the legal treatment accorded to one who commits suicide and a person who assists him has its basis in the moral distinction underlying both acts. In *Bland*, Lord Hoffman noted that the sanctity of life "entails its inviolability by an outsider. Subject to exceptions such as self-defence, human life is inviolate even if the person in question has consented to its violation. That is why although suicide is not a crime, assisting someone to commit suicide is".[7] Accordingly, the intervention of another party places the conduct in a different category than that which only involved the act of the person committing suicide. The reasons for this were laid down by the Supreme Court in *R (on the application of Nicklinson and another) v Ministry of Justice R (on the application of AM) v Director of Public Prosecutions*.[8] The case concerned one Tony Nicklinson who suffered a

[5] Law Commission (2006), p. 145.

[6] Law Commission (2006), p. 145.

[7] 1 All ER 821, p. 831.

[8] [2014] UKSC 38, para 215.

catastrophic stroke, which rendered him completely paralysed, save for movement of his head and eyes. For many years, he had wanted to end his life but could not do so without assistance. Mr. Nicklinson applied to the court in the first instance for a declaration that it would be lawful for a doctor to kill him or to assist him in terminating his life or, if that was refused, (ii) a declaration that the current state of the law in such matter was incompatible with his right to a private life under Article 8 of the ECHR.[9] His application was eventually dismissed at all levels of appeal. The judgement of the Supreme Court in addressing the difference between an act of suicide and assisted suicide can be summarised as follows:

(a) A third party assisting in a suicide is to a larger extent detached from the extreme emotional state experienced by the person wishing to die.
(b) The right of a person who wishes to end his own life is grounded in the principle of autonomy, and such right exists irrespective of the reasons for his decision. The right of a third party assisting the suicide cannot be justified by the same principle, but rather on the merits of compassion, which is very subjective.
(c) The danger of permitting a third party to assist in a suicide allows room for potential abuse, in that he may manipulate and assist others who are more vulnerable to end their lives, also known as the "slippery slope" argument.

Following the coming into force of the Human Rights Act 1998, the compatibility between the prohibition on assisted suicide and Convention rights was considered in *R (on the application of Pretty) v Director of Public Prosecutions*.[10] The patient, who was in the advanced stages of motor neurone disease, wished for her husband to assist in ending her life so that she may be spared the suffering and loss of dignity caused by her illness. She was unsuccessful in obtaining an undertaking from the Director of Public Prosecutions that her husband would not be prosecuted if he assisted her suicide and accordingly challenged the prohibition on the basis that it infringed her rights under the European Convention on Human Rights.

The House of Lords rejected her claim. It held that Article 2 protected the right to life and could not be interpreted as conferring a right to die.[11] Nor did the prohibition on assisted suicide amount to inhumane or degrading treatment, unjustified interference with freedom of thought or discriminatory treatment. When the case was brought before the European Court of Human Rights, the court accepted that the right to respect for private life under Article 8 was broad enough to include

[9] The High Court refused to grant Mr. Nicklinson's declaratory reliefs, and when he eventually passed away due to pneumonia, his wife was added as a party to the proceedings and filed an appeal. At the Court of Appeal, Mr. Lamb was added as a claimant, seeking the same relief to allow him to end his life with assistance, after suffering irreversible paralysis due to a car crash in 1991. His case was similarly unsuccessful.

[10] [2001] UKHL 61.

[11] The first limb of Article 2 of the ECHR on "Right to life" provides: "Everyone's right to life shall be protected by law. No one shall be deprived of his life intentionally save in the execution of a sentence of a court following his conviction of a crime for which this penalty is provided by law".

personal autonomy and physical and psychological integrity.[12] Nevertheless, it held that the interference with that right was justified as necessary for the protection of vulnerable persons and the wider public interest. The significance of *Pretty* therefore lies in the recognition that autonomy-based claims at the end of life may engage fundamental rights while at the same time affirming that such claims do not, without legislative authorisation, displace the criminal prohibition on assisted suicide.

The most significant judicial development related to the judicial approach on assisted suicide is the landmark case of *Nicklinson*, which has been earlier mentioned. The case, which went up to the Supreme Court, discussed the current legal position on the law relating to euthanasia and in particular addressed at length the issue of incompatibility which had been previously raised in *Pretty*.

The court in *Nicklinson,* in referring to *Pretty v UK*[13] and other recent cases similarly decided by the European Court, recognised the validity of the moral and legal contentions on personal autonomy and was unanimous in finding that Section 2 of the Suicide Act engaged article 8 of the ECHR, as it prevented individuals who were physically unable to commit suicide without assistance from exercising their right to self-determination in making end-of-life choices. Such an interference would only be justified if it satisfied the requirements of Article 8(2), i.e. if it is "necessary in a democratic society" for one or more of the purposes specified in that article, which in the context of this case would be "for the prevention of disorder or crime, for the protection of health or morals, or for the protection of the rights and freedoms of others".

Although the Supreme Court agreed that it had the constitutional jurisdiction to make a declaration that the current universal ban on assisted suicide infringed the right conferred under Article 8, the judges were divided on whether it was necessary that declaration of incompatibility should be made at such juncture. The majority were of the view that the facts of the case did not provide them with the essential evidence to justify such a conclusion, and it was more appropriate for the court to allow Parliament to decide on the position and issues involved. Two out of the nine judges who presided, Lady Hale and Lord Kerr, however, dissented on that point and were prepared to issue a declaration of incompatibility. According to Lady Hale, as a general rule, the prohibition against assisting acts of suicide was justified; however, it was the fact that it did not provide any exception for those who were capable of making a voluntary and fully informed decision to end their lives but required help to do so that rendered it incompatible.[14] The Supreme Court therefore stopped short of issuing a declaration of incompatibility but made it clear that they expected Parliament to debate on the matter in the near future. It was however indicated that if Parliament did not rise to the occasion and address the issues raised in

---

[12] Article 8(1) states:

"Right to respect for private and family life

Everyone has the right to respect for his private and family life, his home and his correspondence".

[13] (2002) 12 BHRC 149, pp. 185–186.

[14] (2014) UKSC 38, paras 317–321.

Nicklinson, there would be a possibility that a future application for a declaration of incompatibility would succeed.

The judiciary has undoubtedly played a crucial and substantial role in developing the law on end-of-life decisions, which entail examination of intricate issues on matters of life and death, and assuming responsibility for implementing them. Nevertheless, as can be seen from the preceding discussion, the courts themselves have voiced their concern that such highly contentious moral issues are better resolved through statutes and that court proceedings were not the proper forum for discussion. Earlier, Lord Browne-Wilkinson in *Bland* pointed this out when he said, "it is not for judges to seek to develop new, all embracing principles of law in a way which reflects the individual judges' moral stance when society as a whole is substantially divided on the relevant moral issues".[15] The House of Lords in that case clearly felt that the general position on the law relating to euthanasia was unsatisfactory and this was further augmented by the rapid technological advancements in medicine. The court further highlighted the importance for Parliament to intervene and have the matter properly regulated by way of legislation, so as to provide a sound ethical framework and establish clear procedures within which the rules may be applied in distinct cases of such nature.[16]

More than a decade later, the development in *Nicklinson* as can be seen above reinforced the observation made in *Bland*.[17] In *Nicklinson*, the court justified its decision to defer the matter for Parliament to deliberate upon on several grounds:

(a) Whether Section 2 of the Suicide Act should be amended to ensure compatibility with the provisions of the ECHR raises complex and controversial issues involving ethical and religious considerations that courts would be very cautious to approach.[18]
(b) The issue involves a choice between two fundamental but conflicting ethical principles, i.e. the sanctity of life and individual autonomy that touches upon societal sensitivities, and in respect of which there is no consensus in our society. Therefore, such a decision must be made by those who represent the community at large and cannot be subjected to the individual opinion of judges.[19]
(c) The legislative process is a more effective way of resolving issues that involve difficult questions arising out of moral and social dilemmas, since it allows for all group interests to be considered and has the capacity to access an extensive range of expert opinion available.[20]

In 2018, an application was made to court to challenge the prohibition under Section 2(1) of the Suicide Act on similar grounds to that of *Nicklinson* in *R (on the*

---

15 [1993] 1 All ER 821, p. 880.
16 [1993] 1 All ER 821. See the judgement of the House of Lords, pp. 867, 876, 878, 888–889.
17 [1993] 1 All ER 821.
18 [2014] UKSC 38, para 116.
19 [2014] UKSC 38, para 230.
20 [2014] UKSC 38, para 232.

application of Noel Douglas Conway) v The Secretary of State for Justice.[21] The Divisional Court in *Conway* decided that it was not bound by *Nicklinson* to adjudge the case in a particular way, because of the situational differences between the two. In *Nicklinson*, the Supreme Court refrained from making a declaration of incompatibility based on the fact that it was known then that there was an impending bill on the subject matter, and therefore the issue was due to be debated in Parliament soon. In *Conway*, however, there was no immediate prospect for a concrete proposal to be substantially reconsidered by Parliament regarding the same issue, and so the court held that it was its duty to consider the case on its own merits. In dismissing the application for incompatibility, the court held that there were strong constitutional reasons as to why the Parliament's stand on the necessity of Section 2(1) was to be respected. The court underlined three legitimate aims promoted by the legal provision: (1) the protection of the weak and vulnerable, (2) the preservation of the sanctity of life as a moral principle and (3) the promotion of trust and confidence in the doctor-patient relationship.

At the time of writing, legislative reform on assisted dying in England and Wales post-*Nicklinson* has progressed further than in previous attempts, with the Terminally Ill Adults (End of Life) Bill passing the House of Commons in June 2025. However, the Bill did not complete its passage through the House of Lords before the end of the parliamentary session. Accordingly, the legal position in England and Wales remains unchanged, assisting suicide continues to be governed by Section 2 of the Suicide Act 1961, and intentional life-ending acts remain outside lawful medical practice.

On the medical front, the professional bodies have not spoken with one voice. The British Medical Association and the Royal College of Nursing maintain a neutral position on physician-assisted dying, and the Royal College of General Practitioners moved in March 2025 from opposition to a position of neither supporting nor opposing assisted dying. These developments are generally explained as reflecting the divided views within the respective professions.

The common law position is therefore instructive for Malaysia in two respects. First, it shows that autonomy-based claims at the end of life do not necessarily translate into a right to assisted dying. Second, it demonstrates that where the issue concerns a fundamental change to the criminal law, the courts have generally regarded legislative intervention as the more appropriate route. This is relevant to Malaysia because questions concerning active euthanasia and assisted dying cannot be resolved merely by professional discretion or clinical judgement but require clear legal standards.

3.3.1.2 Addressing the "Slippery Slope Argument"

Another major contention in the legalisation of assisted dying is what is often cited by courts and ethicists as the "slippery slope" argument. According to this view, there is grave concern that if Parliament were to decriminalise or relax the

[21] [2017] EWHC 2447.

prohibition on assisted suicide, this would inevitably lead to arbitrary practices against vulnerable patients who are unable to choose for themselves, such as the elderly, disabled and the mentally ill. In other words, it is feared that the legalisation of assisted dying would cause the practice of nonvoluntary euthanasia to be rampant, as doctors and society as a whole would become desensitised towards the practice of euthanasia as a whole. The following statement in the House of Lords Select Committee Report on Medical Ethics highlights the concern that vulnerable patients, due to their dependency on others, may feel pressured to seek an early death if assisted suicide were to be made legal:

"Issues of life and death do not lend themselves to clear definition, and without that it would be impossible to ensure that it would be possible to frame adequate safeguards against non-voluntary euthanasia were voluntary euthanasia to be legalised. It would be next to impossible to ensure that all acts of euthanasia were truly voluntary, and that liberalisation of the law was not abused".[22]

Those who oppose the legalisation of assisted dying accordingly argue that once the prohibition is relaxed, it may be difficult to confine the practice to the intended category of patients. The concern is that vulnerable persons, particularly those who are elderly, disabled, terminally ill or dependent upon others, may feel pressured to seek an early death because they perceive themselves to be a burden. This concern was articulated in *Nicklinson*, where Lord Sumption warned that the legalisation of assisted suicide may lead to its progressive normalisation among the very old or very ill.[23]

Proponents of reform, however, argue that the risk of abuse may be addressed through carefully designed safeguards, including requirements of mental capacity, voluntariness, absence of undue influence, full information and physical inability to carry out the decision without assistance. While some permissive jurisdictions have not produced conclusive evidence that vulnerable groups are being pressured into assisted dying,[24] the absence of such evidence does not wholly eliminate the risk. As Lord Neuberger observed in *Nicklinson*, negative evidence is often difficult to obtain, and the experience of other jurisdictions may not necessarily translate neatly into another legal and social context.[25]

In the Malaysian context, the slippery slope argument carries particular significance because end-of-life decisions are made within a social setting in which family involvement, religious belief, cultural expectations and vulnerability in illness may strongly influence the patient's expressed wishes. The concern is not merely whether safeguards can be designed in abstract terms, but whether they can operate effectively in a healthcare environment where patients may defer to family members, avoid expressing distress openly or feel themselves to be a burden. For this reason, the common law caution in this area provides a useful reminder that legal reform on

---

[22] House of Lords (1994), p. 49.

[23] [2014] UKSC 38, para 228.

[24] See Commission on Assisted Dying (2012), pp. 138–159.

[25] [2014] UKSC 38, para 88.

intentional life-ending acts requires careful attention to local social and cultural realities.

3.3.2 Legal Justifications for Withholding and Withdrawal of Treatment

The withholding and withdrawal of treatment at the end of life are widely recognised by the courts as a legitimate course of action in medical practice. Where medical treatment no longer provides a patient with quality of life, and the patient's life is merely prolonged through artificial means or technology, it is ethically acceptable for him be allowed to die with decency and dignity. Consequently, the courts have ruled that withholding and withdrawal of futile treatment is not tantamount to a decision to cause death based on several common legal justifications, which will be discussed in turn.

This distinction is particularly important for Malaysia because withholding and withdrawal of life-sustaining treatment remain insufficiently articulated in statutory form. The common law principles discussed below are therefore relevant in clarifying why a decision to discontinue non-beneficial treatment should not be treated in the same manner as an intentional act to cause death, provided that the decision is made in good faith, in the patient's best interests and in accordance with proper professional standards.

3.3.2.1 The "Act-Omission" Distinction

The distinction between "acts" and "omissions" has been the subject of debate not only among ethicists but also those entrusted with judicial authority, in determining legality of withholding and withdrawal of treatment. According to the act-omission distinction, the deliberate commission of an act resulting in harm is generally regarded as more morally and legally culpable than a failure to act, even where the harmful consequences are identical and foreseeable. In this context, actively causing a person's death is considered more blameworthy than passively allowing death to occur. Therefore, acting to kill a patient, even for good reasons, may seem wrong, whereas omitting to act by withholding life-saving treatment may, in certain compelling circumstances, seem right.

The limits of liability in the case of criminal omissions are intrinsically linked to the concept of duty. The law punishes only those who are under a legal duty to act. In general, at common law, a person who affirmatively commits an act with the intention to inflict harm will be subjected to penal consequences. But an intentional omission to act which results in harm to another does not ipso facto amount to an offence, unless the perpetrator, in such relation to the victim, stands under a duty to act. Thus, a person who has a duty to prevent harm and breaches it commits a crime and is punishable under common law. This was one of the principal issues that arose for discussion in *Bland*, where the court sought to distinguish between "the commission of an act which causes death and the omission to do an act which would have prevented death".[26] The court agreed with the submission that because it was not in the patient's best interests to continue receiving life-sustaining treatment, the doctors were under no legal duty to continue with such treatment, and accordingly the decision to withdraw it would not render the latter criminally liable. There was no unlawful omission and, thus, the actus reus (the criminal conduct) in this case had not been made out.

Consequently, the majority of judges held that there was a crucial difference between a doctor who injects a lethal substance which kills the patient and a doctor who withdraws life support and allows his patient to die. In the first situation, the doctor commits an unlawful act and is guilty of murder, while in the latter case, the doctor is not criminally liable because it is essentially an omission and not a breach of duty by the doctor because he is not obliged to continue administering futile treatment. The court, in admitting that it might be difficult to label the doctor's act of discontinuing treatment as an omission, since it would necessarily include some positive measure to stop the life support, sought to justify this by drawing a distinction in the manner of intervention involved. By withdrawing life-sustaining treatment, a doctor is refraining from artificially prolonging the patient's life and decides to allow death to take place naturally, instead of intervening in the natural course of events. This is as opposed to introducing an external agency of death in the form of a lethal injection, where what the doctor is doing is instead an intervention which stops nature from running its own course, resulting in the patient's premature death. Further, the court held that the distinction was substantiated by the fact that while the withdrawal of life-sustaining treatment may be consistent with the doctor's duty of care towards his patient, the law does not recognise it to be a duty of the doctor to actively assist the patient to die to end his suffering.

It is important to note that in *Bland*, the withdrawal of treatment involved the removal of a nasogastric tube which was used to supply artificial nutrition and hydration to the PVS patient. The court recognised the ethical complexity in such a procedure but held that the discontinuance of artificial feeding was similar to the withdrawal of a ventilator and formed part of the regime on medical care and treatment; it should not be seen solely as a means of providing nourishment to the patient. The court was satisfied that in his condition, the continuous supply of artificial nutrition and hydration did not accord the patient with any therapeutic, medical or other forms of benefit, and therefore it was in his best interests for the nasogastric tube to be withdrawn. For the reasons stated in the foregoing paragraphs, the court found that the cessation of artificial feeding was not illegal. Accordingly, where a doctor's treatment of his patient was lawful, the patient's consequent death would be exclusively attributable to the underlying injury or disease from which he or she suffered.[27]

[26] [1993] 1 All ER 821, per Lord Browne-Wilkinson at 880.

[27] [1993] 1 All ER 821, p. 868.

Evidently even within *Bland*, the classification of the withdrawal of life-sustaining treatment from incompetent patients as an "omission" did not sit well with some judges. Lord Browne Wilkinson at the end of his judgement admitted that it was difficult to justify the moral difference between allowing a patient to die slowly by removing therapy which prolongs his life with ending his or her life immediately by lethal injection. Lord Mustill articulated this concern further and opined that reliance upon the "act-omission" distinction in the present situation left the law "morally and intellectually misshapen".[28] Ethically, taking active steps to terminate the life of a suffering patient and withholding him from life-sustaining treatment which will result in his death were indistinguishable, as both involved the intentional termination of the patient's life albeit by way of different methods. Both judges, however, conceded that the court was bound by the law on criminal omissions and accordingly held that since there was no longer a duty to provide invasive medical care and treatment, the omission to do so would not be a breach of criminal law. The aforementioned judicial observation finds its support in the writings of ethicists such as Keown and Kuhse who aver that the *Bland* case appears to have legalised "passive euthanasia", i.e. the hastening of death by omission.[29]

The enactment of the Human Rights Act in 1998 meant that the substance of the common law principles laid down in *Bland* had to be scrutinised in the light of this new piece of legislation. The opportunity to do so arose in the case of *NHS Trust A v M; NHS Trust B v H*,[30] which bore similar facts to *Bland*. In that case, the court was tasked with interpreting Articles 2 and 3[31] of the ECHR to determine whether withdrawal of artificial nutrition and hydration from patients in a persistent vegetative state violated the right to life and prohibition on torture and degrading treatment, respectively. In its judgement, the court held that the context of deprivation of life under Article 2 "must import a deliberate act, as opposed to an omission, by someone acting on behalf of the state, which results in death".[32] A responsible decision by a medical team not to provide treatment was an omission to act and therefore could not amount to intentional deprivation of life by the state. On whether Article 2 conferred a positive obligation on the state to take appropriate measures to protect life, it was held that such an obligation was not absolute. The application of Article 2 in this case would impose a positive obligation to give life-sustaining treatment in circumstances where, according to responsible medical opinion, such treatment was in the best interests of the patient but would not operate to confer an absolute obligation to treat if such treatment would be futile. In summary, it was

[28] [1993] 1 All ER 821, p. 885.

[29] See Keown (2003), pp. 74–82, and Kuhse (1981), pp. 74–82.

[30] [2001] 1 All ER 801.

[31] Article 3 of the ECHR states the prohibition on torture: "No one shall be subjected to torture or to inhuman or degrading treatment or punishment".

[32] *NHS Trust A v M; NHS Trust B v H* [2001] 1 All ER 801, p. 809.

held that the principles laid down in *Bland* were entirely consistent with the provisions of the Human Rights Act 1998.[33] The decision in *Bland* has been consistently applied in subsequent cases and recently affirmed by *Nicklinson* to represent the current common law position where discontinuance of invasive procedures from incompetent patients is concerned.

In Australia, whether withholding or withdrawing treatment constitutes an unlawful omission is connected with the duty to provide the necessaries of life, in so far as it concerns incompetent patients. According to the common law, this duty arises and is incumbent upon a person who voluntarily assumes responsibility for another who is physically or mentally unable to care for himself.[34] A doctor, in treating a patient who is incapable of exercising his autonomous rights, is bound by this common law precept, and therefore failure to provide the necessaries of life would render him liable in breach of such duty. In some Australian jurisdictions, such as Queensland and Western Australia, this common law obligation has been incorporated in their respective penal laws.[35]

The determination of liability must necessarily involve a consideration of whether the medical treatment in question is to be construed as a necessary of life. In the New Zealand case of *Auckland Area Health Board v Attorney General*,[36] the issue before the court was whether artificial respiration could be discontinued from the patient who was suffering from Guillain-Barre syndrome, resulting him being in a "locked-in" and "locked-out" state and completely dependent on ventilatory support. The court held that the ventilator could be regarded as a necessary of life "where it is required to prevent, cure or alleviate a disease that endangers the health or life of the patient".[37] However, since the patient was surviving solely by virtue of such medical intervention and there was no prospect for recovery, the provision of artificial respiration could not properly constitute a necessary of life, and therefore

[33] The court also addressed the implications of Article 3 of the ECHR to the proposed withdrawal of treatment and ruled that such medical procedure did not amount to torture or degrading treatment on the following grounds: (a) it was a decision that was formed upon considerable deliberation by a responsible team of medical experts in the best interests of the patients; and (b) Article 3 requires the victim to be aware of the inhumane or degrading treatment that he or she is experiencing. An insensate patient has no mental consciousness of the treatment that is accorded to him or her, and accordingly in such a case, Article 3 would not apply.

[34] *R v Taktak* 14 (1988) NSWLR 266.

[35] For instance, Section 285 of the Queensland Criminal Code Act 1899 and Section 262 of the Western Australia Criminal Code Act Compilation Act 1913 (both of which are identical):

"...Duty to provide necessaries

It is the duty of every person having charge of another who is unable by reason of age, sickness, unsoundness of mind, detention, or any other cause, to withdraw himself or herself from such charge, and who is unable to provide himself or herself with the necessaries of life, whether the charge is undertaken under a contract, or is imposed by law, or arises by reason of any act, whether lawful or unlawful, of the person who has such charge, to provide for that other person the necessaries of life; and the person is held to have caused any consequences which result to the life or health of the other person by reason of any omission to perform that duty".

[36] [1993] 1 NZLR 235.

[37] [1993] 1 NZLR 235, p. 249.

the doctor was not under a duty to continue the provision of such therapy. The court averred that such a construction depended on each particular set of facts; conversely in situations where the life-sustaining treatment served a medical or therapeutic function, it could possibly be regarded as a necessary of life. Accordingly, a finding of futility precludes the treatment as a necessary of life and removes a doctor's obligation to treat.

The *Bland* case also highlighted the judicial concern that a body of law with respect to issues relating to end-of-life decisions had yet to be developed and that this was a matter that should rightfully be addressed by the Parliament instead of a court of law. Thus, until a proper regulatory framework was established, doctors would need to refer each case involving the proposed withholding or withdrawal of life-sustaining therapy in respect of incompetent patients to the court by way of a declaratory relief. This need for judicial referral, however, was recently revisited in *An NHS Trust and others v Y and another.*[38] Lady Hale, in presiding over the Supreme Court, held that the situation in *Bland* was now a well-established feature of medical practice, and currently there exists proper professional guidance which provided doctors with a decision-making model on the withholding and withdrawal of life-sustaining treatments from incompetent patients. The court considered such professional guidance to constitute part of the present regulatory framework and accordingly ruled that if the relevant guidance was observed and there was no dispute as to what would be in the best interests of the patient, the withholding or withdrawal of treatment could be carried out without necessitating prior judicial sanction. This did not however preclude the role of the court to hear an application should a disagreement arise or if the parties decide to seek judicial assistance.

The position after *An NHS Trust v Y* has more recently been considered in *Townsend v Epsom and St Helier University Hospitals NHS Trust*,[39] where the Court of Appeal reaffirmed that decisions concerning life-sustaining treatment for adults lacking capacity remain subject to the best interests framework under the Mental Capacity Act 2005. While a court application will not be necessary where the relevant parties agree that withdrawal is in the patient's best interests and proper guidance has been followed, unresolved disagreement should be referred to the Court of Protection. The decision is therefore a useful reminder that clinical judgement remains important, but it does not wholly displace the statutory best interests inquiry.

It has been suggested that in terms of the decision-making process with regard to withholding or withdrawal of treatment, Australian case law appears to have vested doctors with greater autonomy than their counterparts in the UK, even before the Supreme Court clarified the procedural practice that had developed after *Bland*. Accordingly, in that jurisdiction, there is no requirement for doctors to refer cases to the court and obtain its permission prior to executing a decision to remove treatment. Thus, finding of futility remains a medical decision. Further, in instances

---

[38] [2018] UKSC 46.

[39] [2026] EWCA Civ 195.

where this has been challenged, the Australian courts have principally deferred to medical opinion and have not interfered with decision by doctors to not treat or discontinue therapy. Such cases will accordingly be highlighted in the succeeding paragraphs discussing on the assessment of best interests.

For Malaysia, the act-omission distinction is significant because it provides a conceptual basis for distinguishing the withdrawal of futile or non-beneficial treatment from active euthanasia. While the distinction is not without difficulty, it remains useful in explaining why a doctor who ceases treatment that no longer serves a therapeutic purpose is not necessarily acting with the intention to cause death. Rather, the doctor may be understood as allowing the underlying illness to take its natural course. This reasoning is particularly relevant in the absence of Malaysian case law directly addressing the criminal liability of doctors in such circumstances.

3.3.2.2 Assessment and Application of the Principle of Best Interests

In *Bland*, the House of Lords distinguished between withholding and withdrawal of treatment from patients who are mentally capable and those who are incapacitated and unable to form decisions. In the case of the former, the refusal of the patient to receive such therapy provides the doctor with a defence from criminal liability, as the doctor cannot perform any invasive treatment unless it is done with the consent of the patient (otherwise, it would amount to the crime of battery and tort of trespass to person). However, if the patient is incompetent, the extent of the right to treat him or her must turn upon the question on whether it is in the patient's best interests to continue receiving invasive care.

The duty to care in medicine is essentially a duty to provide treatment that would be in the best interests of the patient. Originally under the common law, the courts applied the same standard in *Bolam v Friern Hospital Management Committee*[40] that was used to determine the standard of reasonable care in cases of medical negligence, in the ascertainment of a patient's best interests. This classical assessment provided that a doctor would have acted in the best interests of his patient if his actions were in accordance with a practice accepted as proper by a responsible body of medical men skilled in that particular form of treatment. This professional-centred standard was later qualified in *Bolitho v City and Hackney Health Authority*,[41] where the House of Lords held that a body of medical opinion would not be determinative unless it was capable of withstanding logical analysis. Thus, while responsible medical opinion remained relevant, the court was not bound to accept it where it could not be supported by a rational basis. The House of Lords in *Re F (mental patient: sterilisation)*[42] adopted the test in relation to the power vested in the court

[40] [1957] 1 WLR 582.

[41] *Bolitho v City and Hackney Health Authority* [1998] A.C. 232.

[42] [1990] 2 AC 1.

to make a declaration regarding healthcare decisions on behalf of an incapacitated adult.[43] The judgement in *Bland* indicated, however, that the formulation in *Bolam* by itself was not an adequate basis and the decision-making process should encompass wider considerations, particularly in the case of PVS patients.[44] Nevertheless, in that case, the judges agreed with the opinion of the doctors that the patient's best interests did not extend to prolonging his life at all costs.[45]

Consequently, the English courts began to recognise that even the *Bolam* test, as qualified by *Bolitho*, could not by itself determine what would be in the patient's best interests. While responsible medical opinion remained relevant, the assessment of best interests gradually moved beyond a purely medical inquiry and came to include wider welfare, ethical, social and moral considerations. This broader approach was reflected in cases such as *Re MB (an adult: medical treatment)*,[46] *Re A (medical treatment: male sterilisation)*[47] and *Re SL (adult patient: medical treatment)*,[48] where the courts emphasised that best interests could not be confined to medical benefit alone. The relevant inquiry required a balancing exercise in which all circumstances specific to the patient were considered, including the nature of the proposed treatment, its likely benefit or burden, the patient's welfare, social and moral considerations and, where ascertainable, the patient's values and preferences. This approach was later endorsed in cases involving both adults and children, including *Re Wyatt (a child) (medical treatment: continuation or order)*,[49] where the court cautioned against reducing the best interests test to any single factor.

The patient's point of view is also imperative in the assessment of his or her best interests. This was articulated in the Court of Appeal case of *Re J (a minor) (wardship: medical treatment)*[50] which was subsequently reaffirmed by the Supreme Court in *Aintree University Hospitals NHS Foundation Trust v James and others*.[51] The latter case concerned the withholding of life-sustaining procedures from an adult patient who suffered from an incurable illness and lacked the mental capacity to make decisions regarding his medical treatment. It was held that the approach taken by the trial judge was consistent with the test laid down in the preceding case law and that he was correct in considering the patient's welfare in the widest sense, which included the nature of the proposed treatment, its prospect for success and the outcome of such treatment for the patient. The court averred that what would have likely been the patient's wishes and attitude to the treatment must be placed in the balance. Accordingly, in doing so, the court had to consult his caretakers or those

[43] In this case, the patient was mentally handicapped and unable to form her own decisions.

[44] [1993] 1 All ER 821, p. 895.

[45] [1993] 1 All ER 821, p. 848.

[46] (1997) 30 BMLR 175.

[47] [2000] 1 FCR 193.

[48] [2000] 2 FCR 452. See also *Re S (adult patient: sterilisation)* [2001] Fam 15.

[49] [2005] EWCA Civ 1181.

[50] [1990] 3 All ER 930, pp. 936 and 945.

[51] [2014] 1 All ER 573.

interested in his welfare for their opinion on what the patient's attitude would have been.[52]

In cases involving children, parental responsibility remains important but is not decisive. The common law recognises that parents or legal guardians are ordinarily authorised to decide on behalf of a child, but this authority is contingent upon the decision being made in the child's best interests. Where parental wishes conflict with the child's welfare, the court may intervene under its *parens patriae* jurisdiction.

This is illustrated in *Re B (a minor) (wardship: medical treatment)*,[53] where the parents of a child born with Down syndrome refused to consent to an operation to remove an intestinal blockage. The surgical procedure, if carried out, would allow her a life expectancy of 20–30 years; otherwise, she would die in a matter of days. The Court of Appeal reversed the decision of the trial judge who acquiesced to the wishes of the parents and held that the latter had directed himself wrongly; it was the duty of the court to decide whether it was in the best interests of the child to receive such medical treatment, and not whether the parents' wishes should be respected.

In *Re T (a minor) (wardship: medical treatment)*,[54] the approach to be taken by the court in such a situation was further clarified. Although a court in exercising *parens patriae* jurisdiction takes over the rights and duties of parents, this did not ineludibly exclude the parents from the decision-making process. The court, in applying the principle of best interests, reiterated that the welfare of the child was to be the paramount consideration. This had to necessarily include putting into balance broader considerations such as the reasonable views and condition of the child's parents upon which the welfare of the child depended.

The high-profile and tragic case of little Charlie Gard[55] cast the prevailing role of the courts over parental rights into further perspective. The case concerned a terminally ill child who was born with a rare and severe genetic disease which resulted in progressive brain and muscle damage. The parents became aware of experimental treatment in the USA which they believed might help their son, but before the trial therapy could be carried out, Charlie suffered several epileptic fits that caused serious brain damage, and doctors were of the opinion that any further treatment would be futile. The parents, however, insisted that their child undergo the experimental treatment and made preparations to transfer him abroad. The doctors, unhappy with the parents' decision, made an application to the High Court for an order to be made, allowing them to withdraw ventilation and provide palliative care for the child, to which the parents objected. Amidst the intense media attention and inter-

[52] [2014] 1 All ER 573, at pp. 587–588.

[53] [1990] 3 All ER 927.

[54] [1997] 1 All ER 906.

[55] *Great Ormond Street Hospital for Children NHS Foundation Trust v Yates and others* [2018] 1 All ER 569. After the European Court dismissed the application made by Charlie Gard's parents, the doctors submitted a further application to the High Court to affirm the declarations made in the first instance: *Great Ormond Street Hospital for Children NHS Foundation Trust v Yates and others (No 2)* [2018] 1 All ER 623.

national pressure that ensued, the court ruled that it was not in Charlie's best interests for artificial ventilation to continue to be provided, and therefore such withdrawal was lawful. Accordingly, it was also lawful and in the child's best interests to not proceed with the experimental therapy. The parents sought to appeal the decision all the way up to the European Court, and on all three occasions, the appellate courts upheld the High Court's decision. The Charlie Gard case has consequently sparked debates on the extent of parental rights over a child's medical treatment and suggested improvements on how the regulatory system should operate in this respect.

Cases in Australia have shown that the courts have largely refrained from interfering with findings of futility by medical experts and are inclined to accede to their clinical judgement as to what would be the appropriate course of action. In *Isaac Messiha (by his tutor Magdy Messiha) v South East Health*,[56] the court held that although it was not bound by medical opinion, the decision as to which treatment regime would be in the best interests of the patient was "principally a matter for the expertise of professional medical practitioners", and it would be unusual for the court to against a unanimous decision by doctors to cease treatment for a terminally ill patient which, as medical evidence suggests, does not have any real chance of success.[57] It is ultimately for the courts to assess the best interests of a patient who lacks the capacity to consent, and the wishes and interests of other parties such as the parents and health professionals, although relevant and may be considered, are not decisive. This was the ruling laid down in *Australian Capital Territory v JT*,[58] where the court refused to grant a declaration to withhold artificial feeding from the patient. It was averred that this could only be done if the treatment was futile, and not due to the difficulty that the medical carers would face because of the patient's psychosis. Whether a proposed course of treatment is medically feasible, however, remains a matter of clinical judgement. *In the application of Herrington; Re King*,[59] the court allowed the doctors to proceed with providing palliative care, contrary to the wishes of the patient's family, based on the medical opinion that the continuous artificial nutrition and hydration would only serve to prolong the patient's life without affording any therapeutic purpose. Even so, the final assessment of best interests lies with the court, and this must be done upon an evaluation of the circumstances and medical evidence produced. In *Northridge v Central Sydney Area Health Service*,[60] the determination of futility was ruled to be premature and inappropriate, and the court ordered that "the necessary and appropriate treatment...directed towards the preserving of his life and the promoting of his good health and welfare" to be reinstated. In arriving at such a decision, the court found that there existed clinical proof contrary to the diagnosis that the patient was in a permanent vegeta-

[56] [2004] NSWSC 1061.

[57] [2004] NSWSC 1061, paras 25–26.

[58] [2009] ACTSC 105.

[59] [2007] VSC 151.

[60] [2000] NSWSC 1241.

tive state and that there was inadequate adherence to the hospital's own policies in terms of communication and consultation with the patient's relatives.

The best interests approach is instructive for Malaysia because decisions for patients who lack capacity often involve not only clinical judgement but also family participation, religious considerations, the patient's previously expressed values and the practical realities of care. In the absence of a comprehensive Malaysian statutory framework on healthcare decision-making for incapacitated adults, the common law approach offers a useful structure for balancing these considerations. At the same time, its application in Malaysia would require careful adaptation so that family involvement is recognised without displacing the central concern for the patient's welfare.

3.3.2.3 Advance Medical Directives as an Extension of Treatment Refusal

One of the central themes in the end-of-life decision-making process which runs consistently throughout the preceding discussions is the significant and compelling deference to patient autonomy. While a doctor is lawfully bound to respect a patient's preference and personal values in administering the requisite treatment, it has been shown that this proves to be more complexed when the patient is incompetent. The conception of advance medical directives was a means of responding to this dilemma and to address the fear that many people have over the fact that it had become clinically possible to continuously be kept "alive" in a state where they have lost all cognitive functions and are incapable of exercising any control over how they wish to be treated. By doing so, doctors would not only be acting ethically in terms of respecting the patient's right to self-determination, but it would also operate to absolve them from legal liability. It is an established principle in common law that it is unlawful for doctors to administer treatment to a competent adult unless the latter has validly consented to such treatment. To reiterate, a doctor who proceeds to do so without the consent of an adult of sound mind would be committing battery. A competent patient has the right, either for rational or irrational reasons or for no reason at all, to refuse any medical intervention, even though the consequence of such decision may lead to his death.[61]

Under English common law, whether the patient has given a valid consent or refusal to medical treatment essentially rests on whether he did so upon being properly informed that it was done voluntarily and whether he possessed the capacity to make the decision at the time when it was made. In *Re T (adult: refusal of*

[61] *Re M*B (an adult: medical treatment) (1997) 30 BMLR 175, p. 186.

treatment),[62] the test of competency as laid down by the House of Lords necessitated the following conditions to be fulfilled: at the time when the decision was made, (1) the patient must have had the legal capacity and possessed the requisite competence to consent or refuse treatment. In other words, the patient must be an adult and must not suffer from any impairment that may undermine his ability to make up his own mind. It is important to note that a person with reduced capacity does not however ipso facto render him incapable of making a decision as to the treatment in question. Doctors must consider whether the patient had a capacity which was commensurable to the gravity of the decision which he purported to make;[63] (2) the patient must have been aware and intended for the scope and basis of his consent to be applicable in that particular situation.[64] In *Bland*, the court drew attention to the need for special care in ensuring that a prior anticipatory refusal could still be regarded as relevant to the situation at hand[65]; and (3) the patient must have known the nature, purpose and effect of the treatment to which he is consenting.[66] This third element was further clarified in *Re C (adult: refusal of medical treatment)*;[67] in order to determine whether the patient has sufficient understanding, it must first be proven that he understood and is able to retain the information given pertaining to the treatment; secondly, that the patient believes it; and thirdly, that the patient is able to internalise and weigh such information by balancing the need for such treatment with the risks that may be involved, before making a choice.[68]

The conditions of a valid consent as set out above are therefore applicable in determining the legitimacy of an advance medical directive, i.e. whether the person making the advance medical directive was provided the necessary information and was indeed competent at the time when he expressed his preferences. In the event that the person does not satisfy the aforementioned criteria for competency as set out in *Re T (adult: refusal of treatment)*,[69] his advance medical directive will not be valid, and therefore any act or decision pertaining to the person's medical treatment during his period of incapacity must be made in his best interests.

The common law principles on advance refusals of treatment were later given statutory form in the UK through the Mental Capacity Act 2005. Under the Act, an advance decision operates as an anticipatory refusal of specified treatment by a person who had capacity at the time the decision was made and which is intended to apply if that person later lacks capacity. The statutory framework reflects the common law requirements of capacity, voluntariness, adequate information, specificity

---

[62] [1992] 4 All ER 649.

[63] [1992] 4 All ER 649, p. 661. A patient who has reduced capacity (e.g. due to a mental illness) may not necessarily be deprived of his capacity to decide: *Re C (adult: refusal of treatment)* [1994] 1 All ER 819, applied in *Heart of England NHS Foundation Trust v JB* [2014] 137 BMLR 232.

[64] [1992] 4 All ER 649, pp. 662–663.

[65] [1993] 1 All ER 821, p. 866.

[66] *Re T (adult: refusal of medical treatment)* [1992] 4 All ER 649, p. 663.

[67] [1994] 1 All ER 819.

[68] [1994] 1 All ER 819, p. 824.

[69] [1992] 4 All ER 649.

and applicability to the circumstances that have arisen. It also makes clear that an advance decision cannot authorise conduct that would amount to murder, manslaughter or assisted suicide.[70]

The Act further provides more structured rules on revocation, subsequent conduct, the relationship between advance decisions and lasting powers of attorney and the formal requirements applicable to refusals of life-sustaining treatment. These details are significant not because they should be replicated in Malaysia without qualification but because they illustrate how broad common law principles on refusal of treatment may be translated into clearer procedural safeguards. The decision in *W v M and others*[71] demonstrates the importance of such safeguards, as general statements made by a patient while competent were held insufficient to constitute a valid advance refusal where they did not clearly refer to the treatment and circumstances in question.

In Australia, legislation relevant to advance care planning, including advance medical directives, is now available in all States and Territories, except for New South Wales. New South Wales remains the exception in relation to a statutory form for future healthcare choices, in which case reference continues to be made to the rules of common law. In Tasmania, advance medical directives are now governed not only by common law but also by the Guardianship and Administration Act 1995 (Tas), following reforms that came into force in 2022. Advance medical directives in the different Australian jurisdictions are accordingly governed by the following statutes: the Medical Treatment (Health Directions) Act 2006 (ACT), the Advance Personal Planning Act 2013 (NT), the Powers of Attorney Act 1998 (Qld), the Advance Care Directives Act 2013 (SA), the Medical Treatment Planning and Decisions Act 2016 (Vic), the Guardianship and Administration Act 1990 (WA) and the Guardianship and Administration Act 1995 (Tas).

The relevance of these common law and statutory developments to Malaysia lies in the uncertainty surrounding the legal effect of advance medical directives. While the ethical basis for respecting a competent patient's refusal of treatment is relatively clear, the position becomes more difficult where the refusal is made in advance and is intended to operate only after the patient has lost capacity. The common law requirements of capacity, voluntariness, adequate information and clear applicability provide a useful starting point for considering how Malaysia may approach advance refusals of treatment. At the same time, the statutory developments in the UK and Australia demonstrate how these principles may be translated into clearer procedures on validity, applicability, revocation and decision-making for incapacitated patients. These are precisely the areas in which the Malaysian position remains uncertain and where professional guidance alone may be insufficient without clearer statutory recognition.

---

[70] Section 62 of the Mental Capacity Act 2005.

[71] *W (by her litigation friend, B) v M (by her litigation friend, the Official Solicitor) and others* [2011] EWHC 2443 (Fam).

3.3.3 *Palliative and Terminal Sedation: Legal Recognition of the Doctrine of Double Effect*

The doctrine of double effect has often been relied on to justify the act of a doctor in administering treatment to provide symptomatic relief, but which may as a consequence hasten the death of the patient. The doctrine states that it is permissible to aim to bring about a good effect, even if the agent knows (foresees) that, as a side effect of that realised intention, a bad effect will follow, provided that the bad effect is not itself intended and that the good effect is not brought about by means of the bad effect. Therefore, a doctor can alleviate a patient's pain (the good effect) even though he foresees that the patient's death will be hastened (the bad effect), provided that he does not intend the bad effect (i.e. does not deliberately aim or plan to bring about that bad effect) and provided that the death of the patient is not the means by which pain relief is achieved.

The principle of double effect was first judicially recognised and given effect by a court of common law in *R v Adams*.[72] The issue that arose before the court was whether a doctor was entitled to administer treatment that would hasten the patient's death. It was acknowledged that shortening the patient's life constituted murder and providing relief from severe distress could not be pleaded as a valid defence thereto. However, the court noted that "[i]f the first purpose of medicine, the restoration of health, can no longer be achieved, there is still much to do, and he is entitled to do all that is proper and necessary to relieve pain and suffering, even if the measures he takes may incidentally shorten life".

It has been argued that the difficulty in reconciling the doctrine of double effect with the principles of criminal law is that it seeks to drive a wedge between intention and foresight, which in criminal law are interrelated concepts. In *R v Woollin*,[73] the court deliberated on the relationship between intention and foresight as the mental requisite for murder. It was held that it was proper for the court to infer the necessary mens rea (the guilty mind) where a person realises that for all practical purposes, it is inevitable that his actions will result in death or serious harm, despite the fact that he may not have desired or wished for it to occur. Accordingly, this had to be considered in the light of all the evidence of each particular case. In spite of the judgement in *Woollin*, however, subsequent courts in several instances have appeared to approve the doctrine of double effect as a common law defence to negate the element of mens rea and relieve doctors of criminal liability. The Court of Appeal in *Re A (children) (conjoined twins: surgical separation)*[74] sought to distinguish *Woollin* on the ground that the latter was silent on whether the principle laid down in that case was applicable to a situation in which a person or in this situation, a doctor, acts for a good purpose which has foreseeable but undesirable bad consequences. In *Re*

[72] [1957] Crim L. Rev 365.

[73] [1998] 4 All ER 103.

[74] [2000] 57 BMLR 1.

J (a minor) (wardship: medical treatment),[75] Lord Donaldson stated that doctors would need to consider whether a particular medical treatment would be in the best interests of the patient, which may have a side effect where death is more or less likely to take place. To this he added that "the use of drugs to relieve reduce pain will often fully be justified, notwithstanding that this will hasten the moment of death",[76] and differentiated this with the use of drugs and surgical procedures where the primary intent is to cause death, which is prohibited and punishable under the law. In his judgement, Lord Donaldson referred to the judge's instruction to the jury in *R v Cox*.[77] In the latter case, the terminally ill patient was injected with potassium chloride, which had no therapeutic property and led to her death soon after. The jury had to decide whether the doctor's primary purpose, having administered such a lethal substance, was to alleviate the patient's pain and suffering or to deliberately hasten her death. The court cautioned that there was a crucial distinction between the two: in the former instance, the doctor would be absolved from criminal liability; on the other hand, if the jury found his main intention to be the latter, then he would be guilty of attempted murder.

In *Bland*, although the main contention allowing the withdrawal of life-sustaining treatment was that it amounted to a lawful omission, the court acknowledged the application of the principle of double effect as an established rule in deciding whether a proposed treatment would be in the best interests of a patient. Thus, "a doctor may, when caring for a patient who is, for example, dying of cancer, lawfully administer painkilling drugs despite the fact that he knows that an incidental effect of that application will be to abbreviate the patient's life. Such a decision may properly be made as part of the care of the living patient, in his best interests; and, on this basis, the treatment will be lawful".[78] The justifiability of the doctrine of double effect in the provision of palliative care was subsequently reaffirmed by the Supreme Court in *Nicklinson*. Common law therefore appears to have endorsed the application of the doctrine of double effect in justifying a doctor's actions in withholding or withdrawing medical treatment and aspects of pain management. Further, although it may be difficult to reconcile the doctrine of double effect with principles of criminal law, some ethicists suggest that the decision of doctors to withhold or discontinue medical therapy may still be justified under the principles of the duty of care and best interests.[79]

The operation of the doctrine of double effect in the UK to a certain extent has a significant bearing on the common law in Australia. Although there is a paucity of case law in which the doctrine has been applied, three Australian jurisdictions have enacted legislative defences which represent a modified version of this principle:

---

[75] [1990] 3 All ER 930.

[76] [1990] 3 All ER 930, p. 938.

[77] [1992] 12 BMLR 38.

[78] [1993] 1 All ER 821, p. 868.

[79] Allmark and Tod (2009), pp. 35–39, and Tur (2002), pp. 219.

Section 282A of the Queensland Criminal Code Act 1899[80] ("QCCA"), Section 259(1) of the Criminal Code Act 1913 of Western Australia ("CCWA")[81] and Sections 17 and 18 of South Australia's Consent to Treatment and Palliative Care Act 1995[82] ("CTPSA"). An analysis of the scope and extent of these statutory clauses can be summarised as follows:

---

[80] "282A Palliative care

(1) A person is not criminally responsible for providing palliative care to another person if—

(a) the person provides the palliative care in good faith and with reasonable care and skill; and

(b) the provision of the palliative care is reasonable, having regard to the other person's state at the time and all the circumstances of the case; and

(c) the person is a doctor or, if the person is not a doctor, the palliative care is ordered by a doctor who confirms the order in writing.

(2) Subsection (1) applies even if an incidental effect of providing the palliative care is to hasten the other person's death.

(3) However, nothing in this section authorises, justifies or excuses—

(a) an act done or omission made with intent to kill another person; or

(b) aiding another person to kill himself or herself.

(4) To remove any doubt, it is declared that the provision of the palliative care is reasonable only if it is reasonable in the context of good medical practice.

(5) In this section—

good medical practice means good medical practice for the medical profession in Australia having regard to—

(a) the recognised medical standards, practices and procedures of the medical profession in Australia; and

(b) the recognised ethical standards of the medical profession in Australia.

palliative care means care, whether by doing an act or making an omission, directed at maintaining or improving the comfort of a person who is, or would otherwise be, subject to pain and suffering."

[81] "259. Surgical and medical treatment

A person is not criminally responsible for administering, in good faith and with reasonable care and skill, surgical or medical treatment—

(a) to another person for that other person's benefit; or

(b) to an unborn child for the preservation of the mother's life, if the administration of the treatment is reasonable, having regard to the patient's state at the time and to all the circumstances of the case".

[82] "17—The care of people who are dying

(1) A medical practitioner responsible for the treatment or care of a patient in the terminal phase of a terminal illness, or a person participating in the treatment or care of the patient under the medical practitioner's supervision, incurs no civil or criminal liability by administering medical treatment with the intention of relieving pain or distress—

(a) with the consent of the patient or the patient's representative; and

(b) in good faith and without negligence; and

(c) in accordance with proper professional standards of palliative care, even though an incidental effect of the treatment is to hasten the death of the patient.

...

(3) For the purposes of the law of the State—

(a) the administration of medical treatment for the relief of pain or distress in accordance with subsection (1) does not constitute an intervening cause of death; and

(b) the non-application or discontinuance of life sustaining measures in accordance with subsection (2) does not constitute an intervening cause of death.

(1) The legislative defences in the QCCA and CTPSA both make specific reference to the provision of palliative care, although the CTPSA further restricts its scope to palliative care administered specifically for people who are terminally ill. The CCWA admits a more general application, referring to "surgical or medical treatment" which is expressly stated to include palliative care.
(2) Elements of good faith and reasonable care and skill are enunciated in all three statutory provisions as conditions that must be satisfied for a medical practitioner to exempt himself from liability. The CTPSA imposes a further requirement that intention in administering treatment must be to relieve pain or distress, a component that is not required under the common law doctrine of double effect.
(3) In terms of the nature and extent of treatment, the QCCA and CCWA states that it must be "reasonable, having regard to the patient's state at the time and to all the circumstances of the case". The QCCA, however, goes a step further to define "reasonable" treatment to be that which is reasonable in accordance with good medical practice (in relation to medical and ethical standards, practices and procedures) for those involved in the medical profession in Australia.
(4) The extent of protection proffered under both the CTPSA and QCCA specifically includes palliative treatment that fulfils all the necessary elements of defence even if it incidentally hastens the patient's death.

It can therefore be concluded from the foregoing observations that a distinct statutory formulation of the doctrine of double effect exists. Although some of the common law prerequisites are reflected in these legislative defences, they are subsumed within different standards of liability. Nevertheless, the underlying principle remains consistent with the common law approach developed in the UK, namely, that medical treatment administered in good faith for the relief of pain and suffering may remain lawful notwithstanding the possibility that it may incidentally hasten death.

For Malaysia, the doctrine of double effect is particularly relevant because palliative measures may sometimes foreseeably hasten death, even though the doctor's intention is to relieve pain and suffering. The common law distinction between intention and foresight provides a useful analytical tool in distinguishing lawful symptom relief from an act intended to cause death. However, because Malaysian criminal law does not expressly provide a specific defence for palliative care administered in such circumstances, the Australian statutory provisions are especially instructive in showing how legal protection may be framed for doctors who act in good faith, with reasonable care and skill, and in accordance with proper professional practice.

18—Saving provision

(1) This Act does not authorise the administration of medical treatment for the purpose of causing the death of the person to whom the treatment is administered.

(2) This Act does not authorise a person to assist the suicide of another".

3.4 Application of Common Law Principles in End-of-Life Clinical Practice

The preceding sections demonstrate that common law principles have played an important role in clarifying the legality of end-of-life decisions. However, case law alone is insufficient to guide clinical practice in the day-to-day management of dying patients. For this reason, professional guidance, care pathways and clinical protocols remain important in translating legal principles into practical decision-making processes.

There have been a number of professional guidelines and policy frameworks in the UK and Australia which address the standard of care and management of end-of-life decisions. In the UK, guidance issued by the British Medical Association and the General Medical Council reflects the legal principles developed in the case law, particularly in relation to non-beneficial treatment, withholding and withdrawal of life-sustaining treatment, best interests assessment, communication with patients and families, advance decisions and circumstances in which judicial assistance may be required.[83] The General Medical Council's Treatment and Care towards the End of Life: Good Practice in Decision Making, which has since been updated, is particularly significant in recognising that while decision-making should begin from a presumption in favour of prolonging life, there is no absolute obligation to provide or continue treatment where this would not benefit the patient or would be contrary to the patient's known wishes.[84] In this respect, professional guidance functions as an important bridge between legal principle and clinical practice.

Other UK developments further demonstrate the importance of translating broad legal duties into practical care pathways. NICE guidance on *Care of Dying Adults in the Last Days of Life* provides evidence-based direction on symptom management, hydration and clinical care, while national policy developments have increasingly recognised palliative and end-of-life care as part of coordinated health service planning.[85] These instruments do not replace the common law principles discussed earlier, but they assist healthcare professionals in applying those principles in concrete clinical settings.

In Australia, similar guidance is provided through the Code of Ethics of the Australian Medical Association, Good Medical Practice: A Code of Conduct for Doctors in Australia, national palliative care strategies and State-based end-of-life care frameworks. These materials emphasise respect for competent patients' decisions, recognition of the limits of medicine in prolonging life, communication with patients and families and the need to withhold or withdraw treatment where continued intervention no longer benefits the patient.[86] The Queensland Palliative and

[83] See, for instance, British Medical Association (2016) and British Medical Association (2007).

[84] General Medical Council (2024).

[85] See National Institute for Health and Care Excellence (2015), Department of Health (2008) and National Palliative and End of Life Care Partnership (2021).

[86] See, for instance, Australian Medical Association (2025), Medical Board of Australia (2020), Australian Government Department of Health (2018), NSW Ministry of Health (2021) and Government of Western Australia Department of Health (2018).

End-of-Life Care Strategy is especially instructive, as it brings together clinical standards, ethical considerations and the relevant legislative framework on withholding and withdrawal of life-sustaining measures.[87]

The importance of cultural and religious sensitivity is also reflected in professional guidance in both jurisdictions. In Australia, good medical practice requires doctors to understand cultural safety, including different practices and beliefs relating to death and dying, while Queensland Health has published specific resources to assist healthcare providers in caring for patients from diverse religious backgrounds.[88] In the UK, guidance on pastoral, spiritual and religious care similarly recognises that end-of-life care cannot be confined to clinical considerations alone.[89] The relevance of these developments to Malaysia lies in the manner in which they illustrate how legal principles, professional guidance and culturally sensitive care may operate together in end-of-life decision-making. Malaysian professional and clinical guidance have already begun to address withholding and withdrawal of life support, palliative care, advance care planning and communication with patients and families. However, as will be examined in Chap. 4, such guidance does not by itself resolve the underlying legal uncertainty. The experience of the UK and Australia therefore suggests that professional guidance is most effective when it is supported by clear legal principles and, where necessary, statutory clarification.

3.5 Conclusion

Healthcare professionals involved in end-of-life care are often confronted with issues that involve legal considerations which are outside the scope of clinical practice. There is therefore a positive need for doctors to be guided in the decision-making process in order to ensure the legitimacy of their actions. Accordingly, this is best addressed by the construction of legal standards, as well as the formulation of a proper ethical framework which may be actualised in the form of codes of conduct, policies and guidelines. The implementation of such complementary measures will contribute towards a comprehensive care pathway, which will have a twofold effect: (1) provide assurance to doctors that their conduct in the discharge of their professional duties will be both ethical and lawful, which would in turn serve to increase the quality level of care provided, and (2) improve the overall doctor-patient relationship, as patients are assured that their autonomy, including personal beliefs and needs, are given due respect and consideration by doctors in forming and making end-of-life decisions. It can be observed from the preceding discussions that the UK and Australia have taken steps to issue care pathways in end-of-life care. The Australian experience appears to have adopted a more progressive approach in

[87] Queensland Health (2022).

[88] See Queensland Health and Islamic Council of Queensland (2010), Queensland Health (2011a) and Queensland Health (2011b).

[89] See NHS England (2023).

terms of having codified the legal standards on withholding and withdrawal of treatment in the form of statutory legislation and, to a certain extent, developed its own common law principles in relation thereto. Consequently, these developments are particularly instructive in jurisdictions such as Malaysia, where judicial authority addressing end-of-life medical decision-making remains limited and the legislative framework does not expressly articulate the legal standards governing such situations. Given the continuing influence of common law and principles of equity within the Malaysian legal system, the jurisprudence and legislative responses in the UK and Australia may therefore provide useful points of reference in considering the legal standards applicable to palliative care and end-of-life treatment.

References

Allmark P, Tod A (2009) End of life care pathways: Ethical and legal principles. Nurs Standard 24(14):35–39. https://doi.org/10.7748/ns2009.12.24.14.35.c7434

Australian Government Department of Health (2018) *National palliative care strategy 2018*. Australian Government Department of Health, Canberra

Australian Medical Association (2025) AMA Code of Ethics 2025. https://www.ama.com.au/articles/ama-code-ethics-2025. Accessed 2 Feb 2026

British Medical Association (2007) Withholding and withdrawing life-prolonging medical treatment: Guidance for decision making, 3rd edn. Blackwell Publishing, Oxford

British Medical Association (2016) End-of-life care and physician-assisted dying, vol 1. British Medical Association. https://www.bma.org.uk/media/1420/bma-end-of-life-care-and-physician-assisted-dying-volume-one-report.pdf

Commission on Assisted Dying (2012) The Commission on Assisted Dying. Demos, London

Department of Health (2008) End of life care strategy: Promoting high quality care for all adults at the end of life. HMSO, London. https://www.gov.uk/government/publications/end-of-life-care-strategy-promoting-high-quality-care-for-adults-at-the-end-of-their-life

General Medical Council (2024) Treatment and care towards the end of life: Good practice in decision making. https://www.gmc-uk.org/professional-standards/the-professional-standards/treatment-and-care-towards-the-end-of-life. Accessed 26 Apr 2026

Government of Western Australia Department of Health (2018) *WA end-of-life and palliative care strategy 2018–2028*. Department of Health, Perth

House of Lords (1994) Report of the Select Committee on Medical Ethics (HL Paper 21-I). HMSO, London

Keown J (2003) Medical murder by omission? The law and ethics of withholding and withdrawing treatment and tube feeding. Clin Med 3(5):460–463. doi:https://doi.org/10.7861/clinmedicine.3-5-460

Kuhse H (1981) Debate: Extraordinary means and the sanctity of life. J Med Ethics 7(2):74–82. doi:https://doi.org/10.1136/jme.7.2.74

Law Commission (2006) Murder, manslaughter and infanticide (Law Com No. 304; HC 30). TSO, London

Medical Board of Australia (2020) Good medical practice: A code of conduct for doctors in Australia. https://www.medicalboard.gov.au/Codes-Guidelines-Policies/Code-of-conduct.aspx. Accessed 26 Apr 2026

National Institute for Health and Care Excellence (2015) Care of dying adults in the last days of life (NG31). https://www.nice.org.uk/guidance/ng31

National Palliative and End of Life Care Partnership (2021) Ambitions for palliative and end of life care: A national framework for local action 2021–2026. NHS England. https://www.england.

nhs.uk/publication/ambitions-for-palliative-and-end-of-life-care-a-national-framework-for-local-action-2021-2026/

NHS England (2023) NHS chaplaincy: Guidelines for NHS managers on pastoral, spiritual and religious care. https://www.england.nhs.uk/publication/nhs-chaplaincy-guidelines-for-nhs-managers-on-pastoral-spiritual-and-religious-care/

NSW Ministry of Health (2021) *End of life care and decision-making*. Guideline GL2021_004. NSW Ministry of Health, Sydney

Queensland Health (2011a) Health care providers' handbook on Hindu patients. Division of the Chief Health Officer, Queensland Health, Brisbane

Queensland Health (2011b) Health care providers' handbook on Sikh patients. Division of the Chief Health Officer, Queensland Health, Brisbane

Queensland Health, Islamic Council of Queensland (2010) Health care providers' handbook on Muslim patients, 2nd edn. Division of the Chief Health Officer, Queensland Health, Brisbane

Queensland Health (2022) *Palliative and end-of-life care strategy*. Queensland Health, Brisbane

Tur RHS (2002) Just how unlawful is "euthanasia"? J Appl Philos 19(3):219–232. doi:https://doi.org/10.1111/1468-5930.00217

Chapter 4
The Statutory and Regulatory Position on End-of-Life Decisions

Abstract This chapter examines the regulatory framework governing end-of-life decisions in Malaysia. In the absence of specific legislation on palliative care and end-of-life decision-making, doctors must rely on a combination of criminal law provisions, professional ethical codes, clinical guidelines and palliative care standards. The chapter considers how these instruments apply to active euthanasia, withholding and withdrawal of treatment and palliative or terminal sedation. It argues that although Malaysian law has yet to provide a comprehensive regulatory framework, the position is not entirely without guidance. Local professional and clinical instruments increasingly recognise the importance of patient autonomy, medical futility, best interests, family involvement, palliative care and advance care planning. Recent developments, including the 2024 Advance Care Planning Guide, the revised Malaysian Medical Council Consent Guideline, National Standards for Palliative Care with Implementation Guide and ongoing mental capacity reform, further indicate a gradual movement towards a more patient-centred approach. Nevertheless, these developments remain limited by their non-statutory nature. The chapter therefore contends that clearer legal regulation is still needed to support patients, families and medical practitioners in navigating difficult decisions at the end of life.

4.1 Introduction

End-of-life care falls under the sphere of palliative care and is positioned towards the end of the illness trajectory. The circumstances surrounding end-of-life care therefore are inextricably linked to the development of palliative care as a whole. In Malaysia, palliative care is considered to be a relatively new medical frontier, unlike in the UK and Australia, where the provision of palliative care and the ethico-legal framework on end-of-life decisions are more highly developed. Nevertheless, there is a conspicuous need for such issues to be addressed to assist Malaysian doctors in treating terminally ill patients. One of the plausible solutions to address these challenges is through the application of professional codes of conduct that govern

F. Alias, P. N. Jahn Kassim, *Ethics and the Law on End-of-Life Decisions in Malaysia*, https://doi.org/10.1007/978-981-92-3625-1_4

medical practice. Such codes and guidelines play a pivotal role to guide doctors in the proper performance of their duties and in Malaysia need to be enhanced to mitigate and resolve ethical conflicts at the end of life. In addition, comprehensive enforcement of such guidelines would be attainable when affirmed and backed by law. In this respect, due to Malaysia's socio-legal history, established common law principles on issues at the end of life accordingly have a significant impact on the development of legal standards in Malaysia, especially in matters which may not be adequately addressed by local laws. This chapter therefore proceeds on a different footing from the ethical and common law discussions in the preceding chapters. Its concern is not to restate the ethical principles that inform end-of-life care, or to examine common law reasoning in the abstract, but to consider the extent to which existing Malaysian legal, regulatory and professional instruments translate those principles into standards that can guide, justify or constrain clinical decision-making. The question is therefore not only what ought ethically to be done but what the present Malaysian framework authorises, requires or leaves uncertain.

4.2 The Current Legal and Regulatory Framework Governing End-of-Life Decisions

At present, there is no specific legislation regulating palliative care in Malaysia and, in particular, the management of end-of-life decisions. Indubitably, the decision-making process must comply with both ethical principles and legal standards in order to protect the interests of medical practitioners, patients and healthcare providers. This impels the need for a proper care pathway to be constructed, which must be supported by a sound ethico-legal framework. It is therefore necessary to look into the current ethical and legal positions on end-of-life decisions in Malaysia, which may be determined by examining the existing local statutory provisions and ethical codes.

The present Malaysian framework is therefore layered rather than unified. It comprises criminal law at its base, professional regulation at disciplinary level and clinical guidance at operational level. This structure explains why the position is not entirely devoid of guidance yet remains short of a comprehensive legal framework governing end-of-life decision-making.

4.2.1 Statutory Provisions

There is no specific legislation in Malaysia dealing with acts that amount to euthanasia. Nevertheless, the legality of euthanasia in the Malaysian context can be examined through the existing statutory provisions in the Penal Code, which is the country's main piece of legislation governing criminal offences. To date, no local judicial decisions on the matter are available, as issues pertaining to end-of-life care are treated as purely medical decisions and have yet to be brought before the Malaysian courts.

4.2.1.1 Active Euthanasia: Murder of a Lesser Degree?

In criminal law, it is axiomatic for the elements of actus reus (the criminal conduct) and mens rea (the guilty mind) to be established in order to prove that a crime has been committed. Thus, it is first necessary to determine whether the deliberate act of a doctor committed with the intention to cause the death of his patient in the case of active euthanasia would amount to culpable homicide amounting to murder under Section 300 of the Malaysian Penal Code. According to Section 300, culpable homicide is murder, if either of the following situations occur:

(a) if the act by which the death is caused is done with the intention of causing death;
(b) if it is done with the intention of causing such bodily injury as the offender knows to be likely to cause the death of the person to whom the harm is caused;
(c) if it is done with the intention of causing bodily injury to any person, and the bodily injury intended to be inflicted is sufficient in the ordinary course of nature to cause death; or
(d) if the person committing the act knows that it is so imminently dangerous that it must in all probability cause death, or such bodily injury as is likely to cause death and commits such act without any excuse for incurring the risk of causing death, or such injury as aforesaid.

Situations of nonvoluntary and involuntary euthanasia would therefore be directly caught under the aforementioned text.[1] However, cases of active voluntary euthanasia which involve the victim's consent would appear to fall under Exception 5 of Section 300, which states that "[c]ulpable homicide is not murder when the person whose death is caused, being above the age of 18 years, suffers death, or takes the risk of death with his own consent". The effect of this provision is to reduce the liability of the act that caused death to culpable homicide not amounting to murder under Section 299, which indicates that although the Penal Code regards

[1] The punishment for the offence of culpable homicide amounting to murder is death or imprisonment for a term of not less than 30 years but not exceeding 40 years. If not sentenced to death, the offender shall also be punished with whipping of not less than 12 strokes. This is set out under Section 302 of the Penal Code (Act 574). An attempt to commit murder is also an offence. Section 307 states that "[w]hoever does any act with such intention or knowledge and under such circumstances, that if he by that act caused death he would be guilty of murder, shall be punished with imprisonment for a term which may extend to ten years, and shall also be liable to fine; and if hurt is caused to any person by such act, the offender shall be liable to imprisonment for a term which may extend to twenty years". Further, subsection (2) of the same provision provides that "when any person offending under this section is under sentence of imprisonment for life or for a term of twenty years, he may, if hurt is caused, be punished with death".

the value of life to be highly sanctified, in terms of blameworthiness, one who kills with the consent of the victim is less culpable than the person who does so without. This appears to have been the intention of the drafters of the Penal Code, who were reluctant to consider homicide by consent in the same light as murder, especially when it was driven by reasons of humanity:

"This type of homicide ought not to be punished severely as murder…In the first place, the motives which prompt men to this offence are generally more respectable than those which prompt men to the commission of murder. Sometimes it is the effect of a strong sense of religious duty, sometimes of a strong sense of honour, not unfrequently of humanity".[2]

It follows that in the Indian Penal Code, which is the model punitive legislation upon which the Malaysian Penal Code is primarily based, active euthanasia is recognised as a situation in which the aforementioned exception would operate.[3]

The element of "consent" is not expressly defined under the Penal Code, but Section 90 sets out what does not constitute consent:

(a) if the consent is given by a person under fear of injury, or under a misconception of fact, and if the person doing the act knows, or has reason to believe, that the consent was given in consequence of such fear or misconception;
(b) if the consent is given by a person who, from unsoundness of mind or intoxication, is unable to understand the nature and consequence of that to which he gives his consent; or
(c) unless the contrary appears from the context, if the consent is given by a person who is under 12 years of age.

Consent under the Penal Code therefore connotes that there must be free will on the part of the person in allowing the act to be carried out on his person, together with the knowledge of the material facts relevant to his decision-making. In the case of *S Balakrishnan and Another v Public Prosecutor*,[4] consent of the victim towards the treatment that caused him the severe injury was one of the defences raised by the appellant. In that case, the victim was subjected to dunking, which formed part of the lesson plan for the Combat Survival Training Course, organised by the Singapore Armed Forces. As a result of the aggravations practised by the instructors in executing the water treatment, the victim suffered from "near drowning with Acute Respiratory Distress Syndrome".[5] The appellant argued that the victim had consented to such treatment because he had volunteered to attend the course, and therefore by virtue of Section 87,[6] no offence had been committed. The court rejected this argument based on two grounds: (1) the claim that the victim had "volunteered" for

[2] Ratanlal and Dhirajlal (1998), p. 1346.

[3] See Ratanlal and Dhirajlal (1998), p. 1347.

[4] [2005] SGHC 146.

[5] [2005] SGHC 146, p. 261.

[6] Section 87 states the following:

Act not intended and not known to be likely to cause death or grievous hurt, done by consent

the course was refuted by evidence from another witness, since it was a compulsory course for military personnel, and (2) even if the victim had volunteered for the course, the victim's consent would only be valid if he had done so with the knowledge of the treatment that he would have to undergo, and since there was no proof that the victim possessed such knowledge, the contention could not stand. Further, consent requires a mutual understanding between the person carrying out the act and the consenting party. A look into the aforementioned grounds that would vitiate consent under Section 90 also draws attention to the fact that in the case of active voluntary euthanasia, criminal liability under Section 299 would only come into operation if the patient consenting is mentally sound. Thus, this would mean that the terminally ill patient must be competent at the time when consent is given, which comports with the ethical concept and legal standards on self-determination under common law. A patient who is unable to exercise effective autonomy due to the impairment of his cognitive functions or is in a state of severe distress emanating from the pain suffered cannot then be regarded to have given valid consent. The nature and extent of the victim's mental incapacity in rendering him incapable of understanding what he was consenting to is a matter for the court to decide depending on the circumstances of each case.

Consequently, a doctor who ends the life of a patient in Malaysia may avail himself of Exception 5 to Section 300 provided that the elements of consent are fulfilled. The consent of a patient for the doctor to end or assist in putting an end to his life would operate to mitigate the severity of the crime, although the doctor would not be fully exonerated from the liability of his action.

Premised on the foregoing, it follows that the doctor would be liable under Section 299 which states that "[w]hoever causes death by doing an act with the intention of causing death, or with the intention of causing such bodily injury as is likely to cause death, or with the knowledge that he is likely by such act to cause death, commits the offence of culpable homicide". Further, Explanation 1 under Section 299 provides that "[a] person who causes bodily injury to another who is labouring under a disorder, disease, or bodily infirmity, and thereby accelerates the death of that other, shall be deemed to have caused his death". This clearly fits the situation of active voluntary euthanasia, and a doctor performing such an act can be prosecuted and may be found guilty of having committed the offence of culpable homicide not amounting to murder.[7]

"Nothing, which is not intended to cause death or grievous hurt, and which is not known by the doer to be likely to cause death or grievous hurt, is an offence by reason of any harm which it may cause, or be intended by the doer to cause, to any person above eighteen years of age, who has given consent, whether express or implied, to suffer that harm; or by reason of any harm which it may be known by the doer to be likely to cause to any such person who has consented to take the risk of that harm".

[7] Punishment for culpable homicide not amounting to murder is stipulated under Section 304 which states that "[w]hoever commits culpable homicide not amounting to murder shall be punished (a) with imprisonment for a term which may extend to twenty years, and shall also be liable to fine, if the act by which the death is caused is done with the intention of causing death, or of causing such bodily injury as is likely to cause death; or (b) with imprisonment for a term which

An unsuccessful attempt of a doctor to end a patient's life is also treated as a criminal offence under Section 308 of the Penal Code.[8] Likewise, in cases of assisted suicide that do not achieve its intended purpose, the assisting doctor may find himself liable under Section 306 for abetment of suicide.[9]

The position may therefore be stated in narrow terms. Consent or compassion may be relevant to mitigation, but it does not convert an intentional life-ending act into lawful medical treatment. This analysis is confined to conduct directed at causing death and should be distinguished from treatment refusal, withholding or withdrawal of non-beneficial treatment and proportionate measures intended to relieve pain and suffering.

4.2.1.2 Withholding and Withdrawal of Treatment: Determining the Legality of an "Omission"

In the case where a doctor discontinues or withholds life-sustaining treatment from a terminally ill patient, the issue that arises is whether this renders him liable under Section 299, since under the Penal Code, the word "act" would also extend to an "illegal omission", by virtue of Section 32.[10] The general rule is that criminal liability is imputed to conduct which consists of a positive act, rather than an omission. The non-criminalisation of omissions is based on concerns of individual autonomy; accordingly to assign culpability to an omission would not only interfere in a person's fundamental liberty to choose, but it would also be difficult to define the parameters within which a person may be found guilty of an offence, as intentional non-doing may assume different forms and be of varying degrees.

There are, however, certain types of omissions which constitute exceptions to the general rule and are proscribed under the Penal Code. The purport of Section 32 is to make punishable omissions which have caused or intended to cause proscribed harm in the same way had such harm been committed by positive acts, provided that such omissions were illegal. Thus, an omission would attract criminal liability if it satisfied two elements: (a) it must be illegal under Section 43, and (b) a connection

may extend to ten years, or with fine, or with both, if the act is done with the knowledge that it is likely to cause death, but without any intention to cause death, or to cause such bodily injury as is likely to cause death".

[8] Section 308 provides, "Whoever does any act with such intention or knowledge and under such circumstances that if he by that act caused death he would be guilty of culpable homicide not amounting to murder, shall be punished with imprisonment for a term which may extend to three years, or with fine, or with both; and if hurt is caused to any person by such act, shall be punished with imprisonment for a term which may extend to seven years, or with fine, or with both".

[9] According to Section 306, "[i]f any person commits suicide, whoever abets the commission of such suicide shall be punished with imprisonment for a term which may extend to ten years, and shall also be liable to fine".

[10] Section 32 of the Penal Code (Act 574) stipulates, "In every part of this Code, except where a contrary intention appears from the context, words which refer to acts done extend also to illegal omissions".

must be established between the omission and the harm. In other words, the question that needs to be asked would be the following: would the harm have occurred had it not been for the conduct of the accused?

The earlier discussion on the ethical and legal positions of withholding or discontinuing life support therapy at common law has shown that such end-of-life decision is considered to be an omission. The issue is therefore whether the doctor's conduct in not administering further treatment to a dying patient would amount to an illegal omission punishable under the Penal Code. According to Section 43, in order for a conduct to be illegal, it would need to fulfil either of the following requirements:

(a) *That it is an offence*

Section 40 defines the word "offence" to denote "a thing made punishable by this Code". In this respect, there are no provisions in the Penal Code expressly criminalising the withholding and withdrawal of life-sustaining treatment

(b) *That it is prohibited by law*

This refers to omissions which may not necessarily be proscribed as an offence under the Penal Code but which are prohibited and regarded as unlawful under other legal provisions. For example, the conduct of a parent, guardian or caretaker who leaves a child without reasonable supervision and neglects the welfare of that child is prohibited and punishable under Section 33 of the Child Act 2001, although it is not tantamount to a crime under the Penal Code. The withholding or withdrawal of life-sustaining treatment is not classified as unlawful conduct under any existing law in Malaysia, instead it is addressed and recognised as a legitimate medical procedure that may be undertaken in prescribed circumstances under the Code of Medical Ethics issued by the Malaysian Medical Association ("CME"), clinical practice guidelines and ICU management protocols, which are further discussed in the subsequent paragraphs. In essence, codes of ethics are imbued with normative authority; they embody the standards of conduct against which members of the profession are judged and are often referred to in considerations of legality. An ethical code functions as a set of agreed imperatives, which may be alluded to in determining the standard of care in a legal proceeding. Whether the CME and such guidelines have the force of law and are legally binding on medical practitioners, however, is arguable; for instance, the CME contains no indication of such intention or effect, rather referring to it as "guidelines for the proper conduct of the doctor practicing in Malaysia" and that it is not intended to be exhaustive. In addition, neither is the CME incorporated into the Medical Act 1971 or any other legal instrument. Therefore, although doctors in Malaysia are ethically bound by the CME, it might not be entirely accurate to predicate it as a piece of legislation.

(c) *That it furnishes a ground for civil action*

The scope of civil liability under this provision encompasses both tortious wrongs and breach of contract. Under common law, a person is under a legal duty to act if he stands in a certain status with the other party, and failure to properly exercise such duty would render such person liable for civil negligence. In other words, an omission may amount to an offence if the person is under a duty to act and fails to fulfil it. Likewise, no person should be held liable for the consequences of his omission if he was not legally bound to act. It is worth noting that the civil standard of negligence has been judicially recognised to be equivalent to the standard of negligence in criminal cases.[11]

In applying the above rule to the withholding or withdrawal of life-sustaining treatment, it must first be established that there existed a legal duty on the part of the doctor to carry out and/or continue further treatment. The recognition that a doctor owes a legal obligation to his patient is an age-old concept that dates back to ancient writings on medical jurisprudence, identified to be as early as the Code of Hammurabi, which states once a doctor undertakes to treat a patient, a legal relationship exists between the two parties, which gives rise to a duty to provide proper medical treatment and care to the patient. In terms of a decision to withhold or withdraw life support therapy from a terminally ill patient, this is made on the basis of medical futility and/or the request of the patient or family members (in the case of an incompetent patient), as discussed in Chap. 3. In view of the foregoing, two inferences may be deduced:

(a) In cases where the treatment would no longer benefit the patient or would cause the patient further burden and discomfort, the doctor ceases to be duty-bound, since he is not ethically and legally obliged to provide futile treatment which would not be in the best interests of the patient. It is important to reiterate that although a doctor is required to take reasonable steps to keep a patient alive, he is not under an obligation to keep the latter alive at all costs.[12] These principles on the extent of a doctor's duty of care have been judicially laid down in common law, for example, in the leading case of *Bland*[13] and *R (on the application of Burke) v General Medical Council.*[14] Consequently, when no legal duty exists, its omission, i.e. the discontinuance of life-sustaining treatment, will not attract liability. It is to be noted that a doctor still owes a duty towards ensuring that the patient is accorded with the comfort and care that he needs during the final stage of his life, which is exercisable by way of proper palliative care. The dying process takes place naturally, and the patient eventually dies due to the underlying illness and not the withholding or discontinuance of treatment.
(b) Individual autonomy is an ethical right which is imbued in and protected by both civil law and criminal law. In the healthcare setting, it is an established principle that the right to self-determination prevails over sanctity of life when the patient is in a position to partake in the decision-making process concerning his treatment. Thus, the patient's consent must be obtained when administering treatment, and likewise, a refusal must also be complied with, irrespective of

[11] *Ng Keng Yong v Public Prosecutor* [2004] 4 SLR 89, p. 110.

[12] *R (on the application of Burke) v General Medical Council* [2004] All ER 588, para. 106.

[13] *Airedale NHS Trust v Bland* [1993] 1 All ER 821.

[14] [2004] All ER 588.

> the adverse consequences. Failure to adhere to a patient's refusal of treatment would attract civil liability for trespass to person and the criminal offence of assault, and therefore conversely, by implication, a doctor cannot be held culpable for doing the opposite, i.e. respecting the patient's wishes to not carry out or stop medical treatment. It follows that the contention that such end-of-life decision could constitute a ground for civil action is one which would be difficult to sustain, due to the above reasons.[15]

In sum, the central question is not whether every omission is legally neutral but whether, in the circumstances, the doctor remains under a legal duty to continue the treatment in question. Where treatment no longer serves a therapeutic purpose, or where its continuation is contrary to the patient's best interests or valid refusal, the legal basis for insisting upon its continuation becomes difficult to sustain. The above discussion therefore provides credence to the submission that withholding or withdrawal of life-sustaining treatment is unlikely to amount to an offence punishable under Malaysian law, as it does not, in the first instance, fulfil the requirements of an illegal omission.

4.2.1.3 Palliative and Terminal Sedation: Does the Doctrine of Double Effect Constitute an Exemption from Liability?

On the issue of palliative sedation, in view of the earlier discussion that carefully monitored and proportionate amounts of sedatives do not operate to hasten the dying process, it is argued that such intervention would not attract the legal consequences under Sections 300 and 299. In terms of terminal sedation, which involves the withdrawal of artificial nutrition and hydration, the deductions in the foregoing paragraphs would apply, on the basis that such end-of-life decision is considered to be analogous to other life support therapy which may be withheld and withdrawn.

Nevertheless, in cases where medical intervention may indeed involve death as a foreseeable but unintended consequence, the doctrine of double effect would still apply as an ethical justification for such conduct, particularly in deciding what would be in the patient's best interests. In terms of criminal liability, it is submitted that a situation involving the application of double effect may be exempted by virtue of certain provisions under Chap. 4 of the Penal Code, which deal with special defences. It is to be noted that unlike Exception 5 of Section 300 which, if proven, reduces the gravity of the offence and mitigates the punishment (from that of murder to culpable homicide not amounting to murder), the special defences, if successfully pleaded, would result in exonerating the accused.

---

[15] Dr. Norchaya Talib in her book, *Euthanasia: A Malaysian Perspective*, avers that it is unforeseeable that civil actions would be taken against doctors in such cases and to consider withholding and withdrawal of treatment as civil wrongs would be untenable. See Talib (2002), pp. 82–84, and Talib (2012), p. 93. As discussed earlier, a doctor's obligation to honour the requests of a patient is an established principle of common law, as laid down in the landmark case of *Airedale NHS Trust v Bland* [1993] 1 All ER 821. Also see *Re T (adult: refusal of medical treatment)* [1992] 4 All ER 649.

One such relevant provision is Section 81 which deals with exceptions based on necessity. According to Section 81, "[n]othing is an offence merely by reason of its being done with the knowledge that it is likely to cause harm, if it be done without any criminal intention to cause harm, and in good faith for the purpose of preventing or avoiding other harm to person or property". The purport and context of this provision is similar to and represents the principle of double effect in that it adopts the approach of balancing the harm between two different outcomes. This is evident in Illustration (a), where the captain of a steam vessel on the verge of an inevitable collision with a boat carrying 20–30 passengers, and in an attempt to evade such incident, incurs the risk of possibly running down another boat with two passengers on board, will be able to avail himself of the defence of necessity, if the latter does in fact occur.[16] This is however subject to the captain's intention, which is another corresponding element that needs to be proven under both the common law doctrine of double effect and Section 81. Under the Penal Code, the definition of "good faith" is set out in Section 52: "Nothing is said to be done or believed in good faith which is done or believed without due care and attention". Medical interventions are essentially carried out by doctors for the benefit of the patient and devoid of any criminal intent, despite the fact that it is foreseeable that such action might cause harm to the patient, including death. Although what constitutes "good faith" is fairly subjective, it is suggested that this requires the person to demonstrate that not only did he have a good intention but that he exercised reasonable care and skill as required in the discharge of such duty. In this regard, the personal characteristics and circumstances of the person committing the act will be considered; applying this to the context of medical interventions, the doctor's knowledge and skills, clinical aspects and compliance to prescribed protocol would therefore be relevant.

Although the management of end-of-life decisions would most likely fulfil the mental element required to invoke the defence of necessity, an issue that could arise would be as to what would qualify within the ambit of "other harm" under Section 81. According to the Explanation to Section 81, whether the harm to be prevented or avoided justified or excused the risk of doing the act is a question of fact.[17] The Penal Code, however, does not limit the scope of this defence to any particular type of harm, whether perceived or inflicted. Thus, although there has yet to be a local

---

[16] Illustration (a) to Section 81 states:

"A, the captain of a steam vessel, suddenly and without any fault or negligence on his part, finds himself in such a position that, before he can stop his vessel, he must inevitably run down a boat B, with 20 or 30 passengers on board, unless he changes the course of his vessel; and that, by changing his course, he must incur risk of running down a boat, C, with only two passengers on board, which he may possibly clear. Here, if A alters his course without any intention to run down the boat C, and in good faith for the purposes of avoiding the danger to the passengers in the boat B, he is not guilty of an offence, though he may run down the boat C, by doing an act which he knew was likely to cause that effect, if it be found as a matter of fact that the danger which he intended to avoid was such as to excuse him in incurring the risk of running down the boat C".

[17] The Explanation to Section 81 states that "It is a question of fact in such a case whether the harm to be prevented or avoided was of such a nature and so imminent as to justify or excuse the risk of doing the act with the knowledge that it was likely to cause harm".

judicial decision interpreting the relevant provision within the context of end-of-life decisions, this may present a possible window for end-of-life decisions such as palliative and terminal sedation to be included under the purview of the protection accorded under this provision, since they are carried out for the purpose of alleviating the patient's pain and suffering. Under the common law, necessity has been pleaded in several cases concerning medical treatment, although the applicability of such a defence remains obscure in situations involving end-of-life decisions. In *R v Bourne*,[18] for instance, the decision of the doctor to perform an abortion on a 14-year-old adolescent who had been violently raped was justifiable on the ground of preserving the girl's life and alleviating the physical anguish and mental suffering that she would endure if she were to get pregnant. In this case, the judge impliedly made out a case of necessity, instructing the jury that the doctor, based on reasonable grounds and with adequate knowledge, believed he was doing the right thing and that he had done so in good faith for the sole purpose of saving the life of the girl, pursuant to which the jury passed a verdict of acquittal. In *F v West Berkshire Authority and another (Mental Health Act Commission intervening)*,[19] necessity was raised as one of the defences by the House of Lords in issuing a declaration that it was lawful under common law for a patient who was mentally disabled to be sterilised. The court held that the doctrine of necessity provided justification for a doctor, to admit treatment in the best interests of a patient who was unable to provide consent. Lord Goff in his judgement laid down the two basic requirements applicable in such cases of necessity: "(a) there must be a necessity to act when it is not practicable to communicate with the assisted person; and (b) the action taken must be such as a reasonable person would in all the circumstances take, acting in the best interests of the assisted person".[20] It was held that in this case, the sterilisation would be in the best interests of the patient, as her mental condition did not make it possible for her to cope with the pregnancy and matters relating thereto, without causing her both physical and mental anguish. In the recent case of *Nicklinson*, which did involve a form of end-of-life decision, i.e. assisted suicide, one of the arguments put forth by the applicants at the Court of Appeal level was that of necessity. The argument was consequently dismissed by the court on two grounds:

(a) It was inappropriate for the court to admit the defence of necessity in such a complex and controversial case, and it should be left to the legislature to decide on such matter. The judicial process was not one which enabled judges to deal properly with "the range of conflicting considerations and procedural requirements which a proper regulation of the field required".[21]

---

[18] [1938] 3 All ER 615.

[19] [1989] 2 All ER 545.

[20] [1989] 2 All ER 545, p. 565.

[21] *R (on the application of Nicklinson and another) v Ministry of Justice R (on the application of AM) v Director of Public Prosecutions* [2014] UKSC 38, p. 40.

(b) It would go against the intention of legislature to develop a defence of necessity for cases of assisted suicide, when it is expressly clear that latter was proscribed as a serious criminal offence.[22]

In other cases apart from that of active euthanasia, end-of-life decisions have been held to be justifiable on the basis of the autonomy of a competent patient, and the principle of best interests when the patient has diminished capacity, rather than that of necessity.

If the patient has consented to such medical intervention, Section 88 may accordingly be invoked to exculpate the doctor from liability. The provision makes it clear that "[n]othing, which is not intended to cause death, is an offence by reason of any harm which it may cause, or be intended by the doer to cause, or be known by the doer to be likely to cause, to any person for whose benefit it is done in good faith, and who has given a consent, whether express or implied, to suffer that harm, or to take the risk of that harm". Further, the illustration under Section 88 provides an example that directly addresses medical interventions: "A, a surgeon, knowing that a particular operation is likely to cause the death of Z, who suffers under a painful complaint, but not intending to cause Z's death, and intending in good faith, Z's benefit, performs that operation on Z, with Z's consent. A has committed no offence".

In the case of an incompetent patient who has not signified any consent prior to his or her incapacity, the second exception to Section 92[23] may be of relevance. The operation of the provision has the effect that a person who causes any harm to another person in good faith, even without the former's consent, does not commit an offence, provided that it is done to prevent death or grievous hurt or to cure any grievous disease or infirmity.[24] There is however ambiguity whether this would be applicable in an end-of-life setting, where it would be futile to prevent the dying

[22] [2014] UKSC 38, p. 41. This contention was not pursued further when the case was appealed to the Supreme Court.

[23] Section 92 of the Penal Code (Act 574) states:

"Nothing is an offence by reason of any harm which it may cause to a person for whose benefit it is done in good faith, even without that person's consent, if the circumstances are such that it is impossible for that person to signify consent, or if that person is incapable of giving consent, and has no guardian or other person in lawful charge of him from whom it is possible to obtain consent in time for the thing to be done with benefit:

Provided that this exception shall not extend to:

(a) the intentional causing of death, or the attempting to cause death;

(b) the doing of anything which the person doing it knows to be likely to cause death, for any purpose other than the preventing of death or grievous hurt, or the curing of any grievous disease or infirmity;

(c) the voluntary causing of hurt, or to the attempting to cause hurt, for any purpose other than the preventing of death or hurt;

(d) the abetment of any offence, to the committing of which offence it would not extend".

[24] Section 89 is a similar to Section 92 but is applicable to the case of children under the age of 12 and persons of unsound mind, where consent is provided by their guardian or those legally responsible for their care.

process from progressing and where the aim is no longer to cure but to provide adequate and competent palliative care to the patient.

The legal question therefore turns less on the terminology of double effect than on intention, proportionality and ordinary standards of competent symptom control. The distinction to be maintained is between treatment administered in good faith for the relief of distress and conduct undertaken with the purpose of causing death. This distinction is particularly important because Malaysian law does not expressly provide a specific statutory defence for palliative care administered in circumstances where death may be a foreseeable but unintended consequence.

Consequently, the limits of the existing statutory provisions as discussed above make it necessary to examine the role played by professional ethical codes, clinical guidelines and palliative care standards in guiding end-of-life decision-making in Malaysia.

4.2.2 Professional and Clinical Guidance as Regulatory Instruments

In Malaysia, by virtue of Sections 3(1) and 4 of the Medical Act 1971, the Malaysian Medical Council is vested with the power to regulate and monitor medical practice. The local medical scene is also replete with a number of professional non-governmental societies, one of the most reputable being the Malaysian Medical Association ("MMA"). As the main body representing the voice of the medical fraternity, one of the prime objectives of the MMA is to promote the integrity and interests of medical practitioners in all branches of medicine and to maintain the professional standards of medical ethics. More specifically, organisations dedicated to the development and practice of palliative care such as the Malaysian Hospice Council, Academy of Medicine and the Malaysian Society of Intensive Care have prepared guidelines and protocols to direct doctors in the provision of quality and ethical palliative care, which encompasses end-of-life care at the end of its spectrum. Several of these instruments have already been considered in Chap. 2 for the ethical principles they reflect. The present chapter examines them from a different perspective, namely, their regulatory significance, practical scope and limitations in providing guidance to doctors, patients and families in the absence of specific legislation on end-of-life decisions. It is useful in this respect to distinguish between instruments that are connected to disciplinary regulation, instruments that are persuasive as professional guidance and instruments that function primarily as operational clinical protocols.

4.2.2.1 Professional Codes, Clinical Guidelines and Palliative Care Standards

Several policies and guidelines which specifically deal with issues prevalent in end-of-life care have been issued by the Ministry of Health and organisations dedicated to the advancement of palliative care, in order to assist and provide proper direction to healthcare professionals in treating patients with life-limiting illnesses. These include guidance on withholding and withdrawal of life support, palliative care, consent, paediatric life support, intensive care management, national palliative care standards and advance care planning. The instruments considered in this section are relevant not merely because they restate ethical duties but because they form part of the practical framework within which Malaysian doctors and healthcare providers are expected to act. Their importance lies in the manner in which they translate broad ethical and professional principles into processes, records and responsible actors. Although they do not amount to legislation, they may nevertheless provide evidence of reasonable clinical practice, particularly in relation to communication, consultation, documentation and escalation of disagreement.

Code of Professional Conduct

The Code of Professional Conduct ("CPCM") sets out the powers of the Malaysian Medical Council to deal with complaints or information on the misconduct of any practitioner, including the procedure for inquiries and the sanctions that can be imposed. Breaches of the limits of conduct prescribed in the CPCM will render the practitioner liable for serious professional misconduct and subject to disciplinary proceedings.[25]

Consensus on Withdrawal and Withholding of Life Support in the Critically Ill

The Consensus on Withdrawal and Withholding of Life Support in the Critically Ill ("2004 Consensus") issued by the Malaysian College of Anaesthesiologists is a guideline which is aimed at facilitating doctors in treating adult patients who are terminally ill at intensive or critical care units and specifically covers withholding and withdrawal of life support.[26] It sets out, inter alia, the basic principles of medical ethics relating to withholding and withdrawal of life support, the categories of patients to be considered for withholding and withdrawal of life support, decision-making aids and steps to withhold or withdraw life support and plan for withdrawal of life support. The 2004 Consensus also explicates the paucity of case law and lack of legal provisions in Malaysia to direct the relevant decision-making process, as opposed to the position in the UK and the USA. It further states that "[t]he decision to withdraw therapy, usually places responsibility on the doctor/doctors in charge of the patient. Much weight is, however, placed on the wishes of the family or legal guardians".

---

[25] Malaysian Medical Council (2019). The disciplinary jurisdiction and power of the Council to impose punishment is mandated in Sections 29 and 30 of the 1971 Act.

[26] Malaysian Society of Anaesthesiologists, College of Anaesthesiologists, Academy of Medicine of Malaysia (2004).

Consent for Treatment of Patients by Registered Medical Practitioners

Clause 3.16 of the Consent for Treatment of Patients by Registered Medical Practitioners ("Consent Guideline") states that in the event of any complaint, the primary responsibility of ensuring that prior valid consent is obtained from the patient rests with the doctor who is providing the treatment. If the patient's competency is impaired, then the doctor should take the necessary measures to identify the patient's surrogate decision-maker and seek his/her consent.[27] In the absence of a suitable surrogate, decisions may be made in the patient's best interests, but only after steps have first been taken to identify a suitable surrogate and such efforts have been documented.[28]

Several other provisions in the Consent Guideline are particularly relevant in the context of end-of-life decisions. Clause 3.13 covers the right of competent patients to refuse medical treatment and reiterates that such right exists without the need to assign any reasons to the decision. The provision further cautions that where the surrogate decision-maker of an incompetent patient refuses to consent to the patient's treatment, and such decision is not in the best interests of the latter, it would be advisable for the doctor to seek an ethical consult and/or legal support, which may include a judicial declaration.[29] Other significant provisions are Clauses 3.10 to 3.12, which highlight the duty of doctors to give precedence to advance medical directives in deciding whether a particular medical treatment is to be administered during the patient's incapacitated state. The relevant details can be summarised as follows:

(a) A doctor must comply with an unequivocal refusal to treatment in a patient's written directive in the circumstances specified therein.
(b) A doctor should determine the validity of an advance directive by considering the following factors:
    (i) Whether it is sufficiently clear and specific to apply to the clinical circumstances which have arisen
    (ii) Whether it can be said to have been made in contemplation of the current circumstances (e.g. whether the directive was made before or after the diagnosis of the current illness)
    (iii) Whether there is any reason to doubt the patient's competence at the time that the directive was made or whether there was any undue pressure on the patient to make the directive
(c) If the doctor is in doubt about the validity of an advance directive, especially in emergency cases, the doctor can treat the patient in accordance with his professional judgement of the patient's best interests until the validity of the patient's advance medical directives can be determined.

[27] Clause 3.8, Malaysian Medical Council (2025).
[28] Clause 3.9, Malaysian Medical Council (2025).
[29] Clause 3.15, Malaysian Medical Council (2025).

Clinical Practice Guidelines on Withholding and Withdrawing of Life Support in Children

The Clinical Practice Guidelines on Withholding and Withdrawing of Life Support in Children ("CPG") contains a concise explanation on the ethical and legal implications of withholding and withdrawing life-sustaining treatment from children.[30] Decisions must accordingly be based on what would be in the best interests of the child, and consent is to be obtained from the child's parents or those vested with parental responsibility. The parent/guardian's right to consent or refuse treatment may be vitiated, and the child may accordingly be taken into protection as a ward of the Court, if the parent/guardian does not act in the best interests of the child, by virtue of the Child Act 2001.[31] In the event of any disagreement between the medical team and the child's parents, the matter may be taken to and resolved at a court of law.

This CPG is to be read together with the more recent Handbook of Children's Palliative Care Malaysia, which provides a more comprehensive and updated account of paediatric palliative care. The second edition of the handbook reflects Malaysia's growing commitment to the care of children with life-limiting conditions and presents paediatric palliative care as a structured, practical and locally contextualised framework to be integrated into everyday paediatric care.[32] It is significant that the handbook expressly addresses end-of-life care, palliative sedation, withdrawal of life support, home extubation, home death, grief and ethical issues regarding end-of-life care. This is an important development, as it situates the earlier CPG within a broader model of paediatric palliative care which extends from diagnosis to bereavement support.

The handbook also recognises that advance care planning in paediatric care should involve, where possible, the child or adolescent, the parents or legal guardian and the professional caregivers. In doing so, it preserves the centrality of parental responsibility while also acknowledging the importance of involving the child in a manner that is appropriate to the child's age, maturity and condition. The discussion on withdrawal of life support is particularly relevant to the present chapter, as it recommends consultation with a palliative care specialist, careful family meetings, discussion of the options of continuing intensive care support, withholding escalation of support or withdrawing care and consideration of the child's place of care and death. This demonstrates that paediatric end-of-life decision-making in Malaysia is increasingly framed not merely as a question of whether life support may be withheld or withdrawn but as part of a holistic care pathway that requires communication, symptom control, family support and respect for the dignity of the child and family.

---

[30] Ministry of Health Malaysia and Academy of Medicine Malaysia (2005).

[31] Under Section 17(1)(f) of the Child Act 2001 (Act 611), a child is in need of care and protection if the child needs to be examined, investigated or treated:

(i) For the purpose of restoring or preserving his health.

(ii) His parent or guardian neglects or refuses to have him so examined, investigated or treated.

[32] Association for Paediatric Palliative Medicine (2025).

ICU Management Protocols

This publication is a collaborative effort between the Malaysian Society of Intensive Care and Ministry of Health. It sets out policies and protocols concerning the management of critically ill patients to guide doctors in dealing with various clinical issues providing competent care and optimal resource utilisation in ICUs.[33] The ICU Management Protocols, among others, addresses the ethical and practical issues in withholding and withdrawal of life-sustaining treatment in the ICU. This includes stipulating the ethical principles imbued in end-of-life decisions and the importance of assessing the patient's competency. In identifying the patient's prognosis and determining whether it would warrant the withholding and withdrawal of therapy, there should be a consensus between the primary team and intensive care team. The patient must be included in end-of-life discussions if he possesses decision-making capacity; otherwise, engagement with the patient's family is necessary. The protocol also recognises that a patient who has clearly expressed his or her wish against the initiation or continuation of life support therapy, including through clear advance care directives, may fall within the category of patients to be considered for withholding or withdrawal of life-sustaining treatment. This is significant, as it provides express professional acknowledgement that previously expressed preferences of the patient are relevant to ICU decision-making, even in the absence of a comprehensive statutory framework on advance medical directives in Malaysia.

The ICU Management Protocols also provide practical guidance on how withdrawal of life-sustaining treatment should be undertaken. A clear management plan is required to ensure that the withdrawal process occurs smoothly and that it is conveyed to the family with an emphasis on maintaining the comfort of the patient. The protocols require pain and other symptoms such as dyspnoea to be controlled, treatments that do not contribute towards comfort to be discontinued, personal hygiene and dignity to be maintained and family members to be given access to the patient. It further recognises the doctrine of double effect in the use of opioids for comfort, where large doses may unintentionally hasten death but are acceptable when used for symptom relief. The protocol therefore supports the ethical distinction between the withdrawal of burdensome or non-beneficial treatment and the deliberate act of causing death. It also reinforces the importance of documentation by requiring all decisions regarding withdrawal and withholding of treatment to be recorded, including the basis of the decision and the persons among whom it was reached.

National Standards for Palliative Care with I.mplementation Guide

A more recent and significant development is the publication of the National Standards for Palliative Care with Implementation Guide ("National Standards"). This document is an important addition to the Malaysian palliative care framework, as it moves the discussion beyond individual clinical protocols towards the standardisation of palliative care services across different care settings. The Ministry of Health

[33] Malaysian Society of Intensive Care and Ministry of Health Malaysia (2019).

identifies the document as a national standards and implementation guide, and it is intended to serve as a foundational tool for strengthening clinical practice, guiding service development and promoting consistent, quality and patient-centred palliative care in Malaysia.[34]

The significance of the National Standards lies in its regulatory function, although not in the strict legislative sense. It provides a benchmark against which palliative care services may be planned, implemented and evaluated. This is particularly relevant to end-of-life care, as the quality of decision-making at the end of life is inextricably linked to the availability of competent palliative care services, trained personnel, effective communication systems, appropriate referral pathways and continuity of care. In this regard, the National Standards may assist in reducing the disparity between ethical ideals and practical realities, especially in cases where family members and healthcare professionals are required to make difficult decisions concerning life-sustaining treatment, symptom control, discharge planning and the preferred place of care or death.

The relevance of the National Standards may also be seen in the need to ensure that palliative care services are not confined to symptom management in the narrow sense but extend to the review of treatments and medications that may no longer be beneficial to patients approaching the end of life. Recent literature on de-implementation and deprescribing in palliative care highlights the importance of discontinuing interventions that no longer accord with the patient's goals of care or which may impose unnecessary treatment burdens. Local Malaysian research has also begun to engage with this issue, as reflected in the qualitative study by Chin et al. on deprescribing for patients nearing the end of life.[35] This development is significant because it shows that the quality of end-of-life care depends not only on decisions concerning life-sustaining treatment but also on the more routine aspects of clinical care that may affect comfort, dignity and resource use.

The inclusion of the National Standards in the present discussion also strengthens the argument that Malaysia has begun to move towards a more organised palliative care framework. Nevertheless, the standards remain part of a professional and administrative framework rather than a statutory regime that specifically governs end-of-life decisions. They are therefore best understood as an important step in improving the quality and consistency of palliative care, but not as a substitute for clear legal regulation on issues such as advance medical directives, surrogate decision-making and the legal effect of previously expressed treatment preferences.

Advance Care Planning: A Guide for Healthcare Practitioners in Malaysia
The Advance Care Planning: A Guide for Healthcare Practitioners in Malaysia ("ACP Guide") recognises that a surrogate decision-maker may be identified to speak on behalf of the person when the person is unable to do so. It also explains that where a person lacks decision-making capacity, clinicians should refer to family

[34] Ministry of Health Malaysia (2025).

[35] See Chin et al. (2026).

members or surrogate decision-makers and where no surrogate is available, consensus between treating clinicians should be sought regarding prognosis and further goals of care.[36] This is especially relevant in Malaysia, where decision-making at the end of life often involves a family-oriented approach and where disputes may arise among relatives regarding the patient's best interests.

The ACP Guide also expressly distinguishes advance care planning from euthanasia. It states that euthanasia is the intentional killing of a dependent human being for his or her alleged benefit upon competent and voluntary request and that such an act is clearly illegal in Malaysia. It further explains that sedation at the end of life is not euthanasia where it is undertaken in accordance with the principles of proportionality and double effect for the purpose of relieving distressing symptoms, rather than causing death. This clarification is important in the Malaysian context, as it helps to prevent advance care planning from being misconstrued as a means of authorising unlawful acts and instead situates advance care planning within ethically accepted practices of palliative and end-of-life care.

The ACP Guide therefore represents a significant development in Malaysia. Although there remains legal uncertainty surrounding the enforceability of advance medical directives, it provides a coherent professional framework for discussing future care preferences, identifying surrogate decision-makers, documenting values and treatment preferences and supporting shared decision-making. Its value lies in its ability to bridge the existing gap between ethical principles and clinical practice while at the same time highlighting the continuing need for a clearer statutory framework on mental capacity, advance directives and substitute decision-making.

4.2.3 The Legal Status of Advance Medical Directives in Malaysia

The use of advance directives in medical care is a relatively novel concept in Malaysia. This could be primarily attributable to the cultural conditions and lack of exposure on the subject matter in Malaysia. The level of awareness, both on the concept of palliative care in general and specifically on advance medical directives, has been documented by local studies. In a 2007 survey conducted by Htut, Shahrul and Poi, it was found that none of the respondents had heard of advance medical directives or advance care planning.[37] The majority were also hesitant to decide on issues relating to future medical care due to religious reasons and were of the view it was premature or unnecessary to formally decide on related matters. A subsequent 2018 survey conducted by Lim et al. found that only 3.1% of the respondents had heard of advance care planning or advance medical directives.[38] The majority, however, were reported to be receptive to the idea of advance care planning, and the

[36] Ministry of Health Malaysia (2024).

[37] See Htut et al. (2007), p. 63.

[38] Lim et al. (2022), p. e048314.

desire to be able to maintain their autonomy when seriously ill as well as to reduce the burden of their families was cited as the two top motivating factors for advance care planning. In a report issued by Hospis Malaysia in 2016, it was revealed that out of the 600 respondents interviewed, 24.7% answered that they were aware that there existed a provision of services "to relieve the suffering and improve the quality of life for patients and their families living with or dying from a chronic illness", and only 17.2% correctly identified it as hospice or palliative care.[39] Further, a study carried out on Malaysian palliative nurses indicated that there was still a lack of knowledge with regard to end-of-life care and poor perception of end-of-life issues among them.[40]

Statistics in a study conducted to evaluate the attitudes of older Malaysians towards advance care planning indicated that the majority were receptive to the concept. [41] Those who were opposed to it primarily justified their response on the basis that they did not have sufficient information on advance care planning and would prefer their family members to make end-of-life decisions on their behalf when it became necessary. Religious beliefs were also cited as a significant reason for their refusal to participate in advance care planning, as they felt that it was a matter best left to God to decide, a factor which is found to be consistent with the findings of the 2007 survey conducted earlier among elderly Malaysians around the same age group, although the latter was conducted in a smaller cohort. Another local study carried out by Koh et al. among a different group of senior citizens also generated similar results, which reported that a minority of the respondents chose not to have advance medical directives and preferred to leave it to their doctors to decide.[42] Despite not being exhaustive findings, it is submitted that the aforementioned analyses on advance care planning and advance medical directives help to provide insight into the perceptions of Malaysians on the subject.

A more recent qualitative study among Malaysian patients with advanced cancer likewise found that spirituality, culturally sensitive communication and the presence of enablers of advance care planning were central to patients' experiences and preferences at the end of life.[43] This is a useful reminder that the future development of advance medical directives and advance care planning in Malaysia cannot be treated as a purely formal legal exercise but must also be responsive to the social, cultural and spiritual setting within which serious illness discussions take place.

In the past decade, issues regarding its importance and calls by the medical community for increased awareness as well as the wider implementation of advance care planning have made local newspaper headlines. Malaysian doctors have voiced the need for advance medical directives to assist them in managing their patients in a more effective manner, especially in dealing with disputes among family members

---

[39] Sekhar et al. (2016).

[40] Subramanian and Chinna (2013), pp. 287–288.

[41] See Lai et al. (2016), pp. 61–71.

[42] Koh et al. (2017), pp. 62–67.

[43] See Chung et al. (2025).

as to what would be the best course of action for the patient.[44] There is also concern among the religious groups in Malaysia that proper guidelines be issued in respect of advance medical directives and the right of family members to decide on a patient's behalf.[45] To this end, some effort has been initiated to discuss the issue among the relevant sectors, which has recognised the evident need for a comprehensive regulatory framework to be developed, taking into account the different religious and cultural views.[46]

These earlier calls have now been partly addressed through the development of professional and policy guidance, although not yet through a dedicated statutory regime. In this respect, the ACP Guide is important because it clarifies the relationship between advance care planning and advance medical directives in the Malaysian context. Advance care planning functions as a supportive process to guide family members and healthcare providers in understanding the patient's values and preferences when the patient becomes seriously ill or loses capacity. The ACP Guide explains that an advance medical directive is ordinarily a legal document recording a person's preferences for treatment, end-of-life decisions and the appointment of a surrogate decision-maker in jurisdictions that provide the relevant legal framework. At the same time, it makes clear that there is presently no such legal statute in Malaysia, although Malaysian professional guidance has endorsed regard for such directives.

The Consent Guideline revised in 2025 is likewise significant. It now uses the language of mental capacity, surrogate decision-making and advance decisions with greater precision than before. It requires the practitioner to refrain from providing treatment where there is an unequivocal written directive by the patient that the treatment is not to be provided in the circumstances which have arisen, subject to the need to assess clarity, applicability, capacity and voluntariness. Where doubt remains, especially in an emergency, the practitioner may proceed in the patient's best interests while the validity of the advance decision is being determined, and the reasons must be documented. This does not amount to full statutory recognition of advance medical directives, but it does indicate a clearer professional expectation that previously expressed wishes are to be taken seriously.

The limited assistance offered by existing legislation may also be seen in the Mental Health Act 2001. The Act recognises that a mentally disordered person may consent to surgery, electroconvulsive therapy or participation in clinical trials unless assessed by a psychiatrist as being incapable of doing so, in which case consent may be given by the person's guardian or relative. In determining capacity, section 77(5) requires consideration of whether the person understands the condition for which treatment is proposed, the nature and purpose of the treatment, the risks of undergoing or refusing it and whether the person's ability to consent is affected by his or her condition. The Act is nevertheless confined to persons suffering from mental

[44] Mageswari (2014, December 8).

[45] *The Star* (2014, December 8).

[46] Yusof (2015, April), Shaikh Mohd Salleh (2015, September) and Raja Aman (2015, September 2015), p. 35.

disorder and does not provide a general statutory framework for incapacity arising from other medical conditions. Nor does it expressly address the legal effect of advance medical directives, the appointment of healthcare proxies or the standards by which decisions made by guardians or relatives are to be assessed. Its relevance to advance decision-making is therefore limited, and this illustrates the broader difficulty in Malaysian law, namely, that existing statutory provisions remain fragmented and do not yet provide a comprehensive framework for capacity, substituted decision-making and best-interests assessment in healthcare matters.

A related complexity concerns the legal status of a healthcare proxy appointed under an advance medical directive. In the absence of specific legislation recognising a lasting power of attorney for healthcare decisions, uncertainty may arise as to whether such a proxy would have authority to decide on behalf of an incapacitated patient. The existing Power of Attorney Act 1949 does not resolve this difficulty. It regulates ordinary powers of attorney, which are generally unsuitable for healthcare decision-making upon subsequent incapacity, while its provisions on irrevocable powers of attorney are framed in relation to property transactions. The Act is therefore incompatible with the nature and purpose of a healthcare lasting power of attorney. This leaves a significant gap in the present regulatory framework, particularly where an advance medical directive purports not only to record the patient's treatment preferences, but also to identify a person authorised to participate in decision-making on the patient's behalf.

The recent announcement by the Malaysian Deputy Minister in the Prime Minister's Department (Law and Institutional Reform), regarding the proposed drafting of the Mental Capacity Act represents a commendable initiative by the government.[47] Official materials under the Legal Affairs Division's *Peta Reformasi Institusi* (PetaRI) platform show that stakeholder engagement on a Mental Capacity Act began in 2024 and that, as of 2025, the proposal had progressed to a roundtable and empirical study stage for the formulation of a Malaysian Mental Capacity Bill.[48] These developments are important because they recognise the need for a clearer framework on decision-making for adults who lack mental capacity, including questions concerning advance planning, surrogate decision-makers and the protection of vulnerable adults.[49] Accordingly, the drafting process must involve rigorous assessment, incorporating diverse case studies and soliciting input from both the general public and the medical community. Such a multidisciplinary and consultative approach is essential to ensure that advance medical directives are not misconstrued as mere procedural checklists, and to pre-empt potential misconceptions or conflicts concerning the relationship between advance medical directives and advance care planning in future implementation.

Consequently, the present position in Malaysia may now be stated more precisely as follows: advance medical directives are ethically relevant and increasingly recognised in professional and policy instruments. They are, however, not yet

[47] Carvalho (2024, May 21).

[48] Bahagian Hal Ehwal Undang-Undang (2025).

[49] Tan (2025).

supported by a comprehensive legislative framework that conclusively settles their validity, applicability, revocation and enforceability, or the authority of any person nominated to participate in decision-making on the patient's behalf. Until such reform is enacted, doctors must continue to navigate the issue by reference to autonomy, capacity, best interests, professional guidance and careful documentation while remaining attentive to the patient's values, the role of family members and the cultural and spiritual context of end-of-life discussions.

4.3 Conclusion

The foregoing discussion demonstrates that the regulation of end-of-life decisions in Malaysia is still at a formative stage. At present, reliance is placed primarily on the general provisions of the Penal Code, supplemented by professional codes of conduct, consent guidelines, clinical protocols and palliative care standards. These instruments undoubtedly provide some measure of direction to medical practitioners in managing difficult decisions at the end of life. Nevertheless, they do not possess the binding force of a comprehensive statutory framework and are therefore limited in their ability to conclusively resolve the legal uncertainties that may arise in end-of-life decision-making.

It is nevertheless evident that Malaysian law and ethical practice recognise the central principles which underlie end-of-life care, namely, the duty to preserve life, the obligation to act in the best interests of the patient and the need to respect patient autonomy. Consent remains a cornerstone of lawful medical practice, while the growing recognition of advance care planning and advance medical directives in professional and policy instruments reflects an increasing awareness of the need to uphold patient self-determination when capacity is lost. Similarly, local guidance on withholding and withdrawal of treatment, palliative and terminal sedation and the application of the doctrine of double effect illustrates ongoing efforts to reconcile ethical considerations with the realities of medical practice.

Despite these developments, significant gaps remain. Local studies continue to show that public awareness of advance care planning and advance medical directives remains limited and that cultural and religious considerations continue to shape attitudes towards end-of-life decision-making. Recent professional and policy developments, including the ACP Guide, the revised Consent Guideline and the proposed Mental Capacity Bill, indicate a gradual movement towards greater clarity. These developments, however, do not remove the need for a coherent statutory framework that can safeguard patient rights, guide surrogate decision-making and provide greater legal assurance to medical practitioners and healthcare institutions.

References

Association for Paediatric Palliative Medicine (2025) Handbook of children's palliative care Malaysia, 2nd edn. Ministry of Health Malaysia

Bahagian Hal Ehwal Undang-Undang (2025) RUU Keupayaan Mental 2025 (Kajian Empirikal Akta Keupayaan Mental 2025). Peta Reformasi Institusi (PetaRI). https://petari.bheuu.gov.my/ruu-ombudsman-2025-6/. Accessed 26 Apr 2026

Carvalho M (2024) Govt working to enact Mental Capacity Act for Malaysia, says Kulasegaran. The Star, 21 May 2024. https://www.thestar.com.my/news/nation/2024/05/21/govt-working-to-enact-mental-capacity-act-for-malaysia-says-kulasegaran. Accessed 7 May 2026

Chin AAH, Lai PSM, McCarthy SA (2026) Deprescribing for patients nearing end of life: Views, barriers and facilitators of palliative care patients, carers and nurses. Support Care Cancer 34:303. https://doi.org/10.1007/s00520-026-10522-3

Chung I, Khoo SY, Low LL (2025) An insight into the experiences of Malaysian patients with advanced cancer and their preferences in end-of-life care: A qualitative study. Am J Hosp Palliat Med 42(1):5–13. https://doi.org/10.1177/10499091241233599

Htut Y, Shahrul K, Poi PJH (2007) The views of older Malaysians on advanced directive and advanced care planning: A qualitative study. Asia Pac J Public Health 19(3):58–67. https://doi.org/10.1177/101053950701900310

Koh TL, Tajudin TR, Abdulshakour Z (2017) Advance directives among elderly population: A Malaysian experience. J Indian Acad Geriatr 13(2):62–67. https://doi.org/10.35262/jiag.v13i2.62-67

Lai PSM, Mudri SM, Chinna K, Othman S (2016) The development and validation of the advance care planning questionnaire in Malaysia. BMC Med Ethics 17:61–71. https://doi.org/10.1186/s12910-016-0147-8

Lim MK, Lai PSM, Lim PS et al (2022) Knowledge, attitude and practice of community-dwelling adults regarding advance care planning in Malaysia: A cross-sectional study. BMJ Open 12(2):e048314. https://doi.org/10.1136/bmjopen-2020-048314

Mageswari M (2014) 'Living will' for the terminally ill. The Star, 8 Dec 2014. http://www.thestar.com.my/News/Nation/2014/12/08/Living-will-for-the-terminally-ill-AMD-gives-patients-greater-say-on-how-they-wish-to-die/. Accessed 7 May 2026

Malaysian Medical Council (2019) Code of professional conduct. https://mmc.gov.my/wp-content/uploads/2022/04/Code-of-Professional-Conduct-2019.pdf. Accessed 26 Apr 2026

Malaysian Medical Council (2025) Consent for treatment of patients by registered medical practitioners. https://mmc.gov.my/wp-content/uploads/2025/09/Consent-for-Treatment-of-Patients-by-Registered-Medical-Practitioners.pdf. Accessed 26 Apr 2026

Malaysian Society of Anaesthesiologists, College of Anaesthesiologists, Academy of Medicine of Malaysia (2004) Consensus on withdrawal and withholding of life support in the critically ill. Berita Anestesiologi 6(1). http://www.msa.net.my/newsmaster.cfm?&menuid=21&action=view&retrieveid=23#ConsensusOnWithdrawalAndWithholdingOfLifeSupportIntheCriticallyIll. Accessed 10 Feb 2022

Malaysian Society of Intensive Care, Ministry of Health Malaysia (2019) ICU management protocols. Malaysian Society of Intensive Care

Ministry of Health Malaysia (2024) Advance care planning: A guide for healthcare practitioners in Malaysia. Medical Development Division, Ministry of Health Malaysia

Ministry of Health Malaysia (2025) National standards for palliative care with implementation guide. Medical Development Division, Ministry of Health Malaysia

Ministry of Health Malaysia, Academy of Medicine Malaysia (2005) Clinical practice guidelines on withholding and withdrawing of life support in children. Ministry of Health Malaysia

Raja Aman RES (2015) Give legal effect to directives. The Star, 21 Sept 2015, p 35

Ratanlal R, Thakore DK, Thakker CK (1998) Ratanlal & Dhirajlal's law of crimes: A commentary on the Indian Penal Code, 1860, 24th edn. Bharat Law House

Sekhar WY, Connor S, McCarthy S, Hamzah E (2016) Palliative needs assessment: Malaysia. Hospis Malaysia

Shaikh Mohd Salleh SMS (2015) Agenda on advance medical directives. The Star, 8 Sept 2015. https://www.thestar.com.my/opinion/columnists/ikim-views/2015/09/08/agenda-on-advance-medical-directives-muslim-scholars-take-the-view-that-there-is-a-limit-to-a-patien/. Accessed 7 May 2026

Subramanian P, Chinna K (2013) Knowledge and perception on end-of-life care, death and dying among palliative nurses. BMJ Support Palliat Care 3(2):287–288. https://doi.org/10.1136/bmjspcare-2013-000491.162

Talib N (2002) Euthanasia: A Malaysian perspective. Sweet & Maxwell Asia

Talib N (2012) Legal and ethical issues in the care of terminally ill patients. J Health Transl Med 9(1):93–94

Tan MKM (2025) Determining mental capacity and identifying surrogates: the need for clearer guidance on medical decision-making in Malaysia. Asian Bioethics Review 17:117–128. https://doi.org/10.1007/s41649-024-00313-5

The Star (2014) Group calls for guidelines on issuance of directive. 8 Dec 2014. http://www.thestar.com.my/News/Nation/2014/12/08/Group-calls-for-guidelines-on-issuance-of-directive/. Accessed 7 May 2026

Yusof AN (2015) AMD: Pesakit tentukan hak rawatan. IKIMfm. https://ikimfm.my/amd-pesakit-tentukan-hak-rawatan/. Accessed 7 Jan 2022

Chapter 5
Building a Coherent Ethico-Legal Framework for End-of-Life Decisions in Malaysia

Abstract This chapter consolidates the central findings of the book and advances the reform argument for a coherent ethico-legal framework on end-of-life decisions in Malaysia. It reassesses the adequacies and inadequacies of the current Malaysian position in light of recent developments, particularly the 2024 Advance Care Planning Guide, the revised Malaysian Medical Council Consent Guideline and the National Standards for Palliative Care with Implementation Guide. While these instruments signify meaningful progress in professional guidance, advance care planning, consent, shared decision-making and palliative care standards, it is submitted that they do not yet amount to a complete regulatory framework. The discussion identifies the continuing need for clearer legal standards on withholding and withdrawal of treatment, symptom relief that may foreseeably hasten death, advance decisions, surrogate decision-making and mental capacity. It further situates end-of-life decision-making within the wider continuum of palliative care and highlights the importance of equitable access, cultural competence, quality improvement and resource-sensitive service delivery. The chapter concludes that future reform in Malaysia should therefore focus on consolidating existing professional guidance while developing legal safeguards on capacity, best interests, surrogate authority, documentation and protection of doctors who act in accordance with recognised professional standards.

5.1 Introduction

This concluding chapter draws together the central findings of this book and sets out the principal agendas for reform. The preceding chapters have shown that end-of-life decisions in Malaysia remain addressed in general terms in local ethical codes and only to a limited extent in existing legal provisions. At the same time, the field has not remained static. There have been important recent local developments, most notably the issuance of the Ministry of Health Malaysia's Advance Care Planning:

F. Alias, P. N. Jahn Kassim, *Ethics and the Law on End-of-Life Decisions in Malaysia*, https://doi.org/10.1007/978-981-92-3625-1_5

A Guide for Healthcare Practitioners in Malaysia[1] in August 2024 ("ACP Guide") and the updated Malaysian Medical Council Guideline on Consent for Treatment of Patients by Registered Medical Practitioners[2] ("Consent Guideline") in 2025. These developments materially improve the practical guidance available to clinicians, even though they do not yet amount to a complete statutory framework.

Accordingly, the analysis that follows retains the central thesis of this work, namely, that Malaysia still requires a coherent ethico-legal framework on end-of-life decisions, but it does so with a refinement. The more accurate question now is whether the present combination of ethical guidance, professional standards and health policy is sufficient to provide clarity, legitimacy and protection in respect of withholding and withdrawing life-sustaining treatment, pain and symptom management, shared decision-making and advance planning. It is submitted that although the regulatory position has developed in a more positive direction in recent years, these developments have yet to fully resolve the need for clearer ethico-legal standards and more coherent regulatory protection.

For that reason, this chapter first revisits the adequacies and inadequacies of the current Malaysian position, before proceeding to the principal reform priorities. In doing so, it also incorporates recent local publications on palliative and end-of-life care, including work on access, quality indicators, clinician perspectives and service strategies, in order to ensure that the recommendations made herein are current and responsive to the present Malaysian context.

5.2 Assessing the Current Malaysian Regulatory Position on End-of-Life Decisions

From the preceding discussion in previous chapters, it can be seen that end-of-life decisions in Malaysia remain a subject matter that is addressed in broad terms in local ethical codes and, to a certain extent, inadequately in legal provisions. A clear inference can nevertheless still be made with regard to the Malaysian position on active euthanasia: it is both unethical and illegal in accordance with the stand taken in local ethical codes and by virtue of the interpretation of Section 299 of the Penal Code. However, the position is not as precise when it comes to withholding and withdrawal of treatment, medical interventions which may hasten death, advance planning and decisions made for incapacitated patients. The more recent guidance improves the practice position, but it does not fully extinguish the legal uncertainty.

[1] Ministry of Health Malaysia (2024).

[2] Malaysian Medical Council (2025).

5.2.1 Analysis of Current Legal Standards

In terms of legal standards, there are still no local statutory provisions or judicial decisions laying down a comprehensive set of principles governing the conduct of doctors in end-of-life decision-making. The Penal Code lies on the other end of the spectrum; being punitive law, it deals with criminal liability and does not specifically list active euthanasia, withholding or withdrawal of life-sustaining treatment or symptom management that may foreseeably hasten death as separately defined offences. Much of the earlier discussion on the Penal Code remains inferential in character, since Malaysian courts have yet to pronounce directly on these provisions in the context of end-of-life decisions.

A clear position may nevertheless be inferred in relation to active euthanasia. Although active euthanasia is not expressly prohibited as a distinct offence under the Penal Code, the combined effect of Section 299 and Exception 5 to Section 300 indicates that the intentional ending of a patient's life would remain criminal, even where consent is given. In this respect, the Penal Code operates as an indirect, but nevertheless important, prohibition against active euthanasia. This position is also consistent with the stance taken in local ethical codes and with the broader religious and moral sensitivities surrounding intentional life-ending acts in Malaysia. It is therefore difficult to envisage active euthanasia being treated differently under the present Malaysian legal and social framework, unless Parliament were to make an express legislative choice to that effect.

The position is less precise, however, when the discussion moves away from active euthanasia and towards withholding and withdrawal of treatment, palliative sedation, pain management, advance planning and decisions made for patients who lack capacity. The Penal Code does not appear to prohibit the withholding or withdrawal of life-sustaining therapy in the same way that it prohibits active measures to end life. Its provisions on good faith, necessity and acts done for the benefit of another may, to a certain extent, be invoked to protect doctors whose actions are consistent with good medical practice and undertaken for the benefit of the patient. However, there remains uncertainty as to how these provisions would be interpreted in end-of-life situations, particularly where death is imminent, curative treatment is no longer possible and the aim of medical care has shifted from the prevention of death to the relief of suffering and the avoidance of non-beneficial intervention.

It is at this point that the common law principles discussed in Chap. 3 assume particular significance. The purpose of examining the UK and Australian positions is not to suggest that Malaysian law should simply adopt foreign principles without qualification. Rather, the common law provides a useful analytical framework for distinguishing between different forms of end-of-life decisions. It explains why the withholding or withdrawal of futile or non-beneficial treatment is not equivalent to active euthanasia; why a doctor's duty to treat does not require treatment to be continued where it no longer serves the patient's interests; and why the intention behind palliative measures remains central in distinguishing symptom relief from an act intended to cause death.

This is especially important in the Malaysian context because the existing legal position does not yet provide clear answers to these questions. Where a competent patient refuses treatment, the common law offers a principled basis for respecting that refusal. Where a patient lacks capacity, the best-interests approach provides a framework for considering the patient's welfare, wishes, values, clinical condition and the views of family members. Where pain and symptom management may foreseeably hasten death, the doctrine of double effect assists in clarifying that foreseeability of death is not the same as an intention to kill. These principles do not resolve every difficulty, but they provide a structured language through which Malaysian law may begin to address questions that are presently left largely to clinical judgement and professional guidance.

Nevertheless, reliance on common law alone cannot fully answer the existing regulatory gap. The experience in cases such as *Bland*[3] and *Nicklinson*[4] illustrates both the usefulness and the limits of judicial reasoning in this area. Courts may clarify legal principles in individual cases, but they are not necessarily the most appropriate forum to determine, on a case-by-case basis, issues that are morally contentious, socially sensitive and closely connected to public policy. End-of-life decisions engage not only legal doctrine but also religious belief, cultural values, family involvement, professional judgement and the allocation of healthcare responsibilities. In the Malaysian context, these considerations make it even more important that any framework should be developed through a process that allows wider ethical, professional and social deliberation.

It must further be noted that the application of external common law principles in Malaysia is necessarily subject to local circumstances. Hence, the racial, religious and cultural demography in Malaysia constitutes a pertinent factor that requires due consideration. Ethical guidelines and legal standards on end-of-life decisions cannot be received from other jurisdictions without appropriate modification but must be constructed in a manner that takes into account the values and perspectives of the different communities in Malaysia, particularly since the subject concerns matters that are highly sensitive and closely connected to the meaning of life, death, suffering and dignity. The more appropriate use of external common law is therefore not as a model to be adopted in its entirety, but as a persuasive source from which relevant principles may be carefully adapted to the Malaysian legal and healthcare setting.

What has changed in recent years, however, is that the legal and professional discourse on end-of-life decisions has become more concrete. The ACP Guide expressly acknowledges that Malaysia has yet to pass legal statutes on advance directives or legal proxies but at the same time frames advance care planning as ethically justifiable and professionally relevant, with the patient's best interests and good medical practice

---

[3] *Airedale NHS Trust v Bland* [1993] 1 All ER 821.

[4] *R (on the application of Nicklinson and another) v Ministry of Justice R (on the application of AM) v Director of Public Prosecutions* [2014] UKSC 38.

remaining central to the decision-making process.[5] In a similar vein, the revised Consent Guideline introduces clearer professional language on mental capacity, supported decision-making, surrogate decision-makers, advance decisions and best interests.[6] These are significant developments. Although they do not create a statutory regime, they have narrowed the practical uncertainty to some extent and provide a stronger professional basis upon which doctors may act in the end-of-life care setting.

Even so, ethical codes and professional guidelines remain limited in the absence of legal affirmation. They are valuable because they are more flexible and more capable of responding to developments in medical practice. However, they do not by themselves provide the same degree of certainty, enforceability or legal protection as legislation. This is particularly important where doctors may be exposed to criminal liability despite acting in good faith, with reasonable care and skill, and in accordance with recognised professional standards. The present reliance on the general provisions and special defences of the Penal Code is therefore inadequate and somewhat awkward, because those provisions were not drafted with end-of-life care specifically in mind.

For this reason, the need for clearer legal safeguards remains persuasive. The present reliance on general Penal Code provisions and professional guidance may offer some measure of protection, but it does not provide the same degree of clarity as a provision drafted specifically with end-of-life decision-making in mind. The more appropriate approach, as considered further below, would be for the law to affirm a limited number of core principles while preserving sufficient flexibility for clinical judgement and professional guidance.

Taken together, the significance of these common law principles lies not in suggesting that Malaysian law should take external common law principles as directly applicable, but in the manner in which they identify the distinct questions that Malaysian law must now address: the distinction between "killing" and "letting die", the legal significance of medical futility, the scope of patient autonomy, the meaning of best interests, the role of family members and surrogate decision-makers and the treatment of palliative measures that may foreseeably hasten death. These questions are not yet addressed with sufficient clarity within the existing Malaysian statutory framework. Common law therefore remains an important persuasive resource, but it should ultimately serve as a bridge towards clearer Malaysian legal standards, rather than as a substitute for them.

5.2.2 Analysis of Ethical Codes and Guidelines

There has yet to be one comprehensive statutory or quasi-statutory framework to assist Malaysian doctors in dealing with end-of-life decisions, although it can now be observed that the regulatory position is less fragmented than before. The earlier

[5] See Ministry of Health Malaysia (2024).

[6] See Malaysian Medical Council (2025).

directives, handbooks and protocols issued by different medical societies and professional groups represented commendable efforts in providing practical guidance to doctors. Their scope, however, remained uneven, and their respective authority varied. The ACP Guide and current Consent Guideline have now improved this position to a significant extent by providing more structured guidance on communication, shared decision-making, mental capacity, surrogate involvement, goals of care and the practical aspects of advance care planning.

Notwithstanding these developments, further refinement remains necessary in several respects. First, there is still a need for a more detailed local protocol on the steps to be taken when the views of the patient, family members and treating team diverge. Second, the incorporation of legal standards remains incomplete, largely because the law itself continues to lack precision on several aspects of end-of-life decision-making. Third, although guidance on cultural competence is now more visible, it should still be developed further so that doctors are assisted not only in recognising the relevance of religion and culture but also in understanding how such considerations may influence decisions on resuscitation, withholding or withdrawal of treatment, palliative sedation, artificial nutrition and hydration, place of care and rituals at the end of life. Fourth, the growing significance of resource allocation and equity in end-of-life care also warrants more express consideration in local guidance.

Recent Malaysian scholarship lends support to this conclusion. The 2025 modified Delphi study on quality indicators for end-of-life cancer care in Malaysia identified a comprehensive set of indicators and highlighted the importance of symptom management, access to palliative care services, care coordination and quality monitoring.[7] More significantly, it recognised that the meaning of quality end-of-life care is necessarily context-dependent and that, in Malaysia, the absence of a legally binding framework for advance care planning may complicate the application and measurement of certain decision-related indicators. This suggests that the existing shortcomings are no longer merely theoretical or normative in nature but may also carry implications for quality assessment, audit and future system improvement.

Viewed collectively, the existing ethical codes, clinical guidelines and palliative care standards show that Malaysia is no longer without practical guidance on end-of-life decision-making. They provide an emerging professional framework on communication, family involvement, best interests, goals of care, advance care planning and palliative management. Their limitation, however, lies in the fact that they do not conclusively determine the legal consequences of acting or declining to act in accordance with them. They may guide the doctor's conduct and support the reasonableness of the decision-making process, but they do not remove the need for clearer legal standards on withholding and withdrawal of treatment, palliative measures that may foreseeably hasten death, advance medical directives and surrogate decision-making.

[7] See Wong et al. (2025).

5.2.3 Analysis on the Current Status of Advance Care Planning and Advance Medical Directives

The central legal difficulty concerning advance medical directives in Malaysia is not whether a patient's previously expressed wishes should be taken seriously but under what conditions those wishes become legally binding rather than merely persuasive. This requires three related questions to be distinguished: first, whether the directive was validly made; second, whether it is applicable to the present clinical circumstances; and third, whether any person named in the directive has legal authority to participate in or make decisions on behalf of the patient.

Malaysia does not yet have legislation which confers binding legal status on advance directives or legal proxies. However, the issuance of the ACP Guide by the Ministry of Health Malaysia, together with the related public materials and the revised Consent Guideline, represents an important development in the Malaysian regulatory landscape. These instruments have moved the discussion beyond the narrower language of advance directives towards the broader and more clinically workable process of advance care planning, in which the patient's values, goals of care, treatment preferences, family involvement and future decision-making needs are addressed in a more structured manner.

For the purposes of this concluding chapter, the significance of these developments lies not so much in restating their contents but in assessing what they reveal about the present direction of Malaysian reform. The ACP Guide and Consent Guideline indicate that advance care planning is increasingly recognised as ethically justified, professionally relevant and practically necessary in serious illness care. They also provide a more concrete basis for doctors to engage patients and family members on future care preferences, surrogate involvement, best interests and the documentation of treatment wishes. This is a meaningful progression from the earlier position, where advance medical directives were only briefly mentioned in local ethical and professional instruments.

At the same time, these developments do not fully resolve the legal issues identified in this study. Advance care planning in Malaysia remains, in its present form, a matter of policy and professional practice rather than a legally binding regime. The current framework does not yet conclusively determine the validity, applicability, revocation and enforceability of advance medical directives. Nor does it establish a lasting power of attorney mechanism for healthcare decisions or a formal national system for the safekeeping, retrieval and institutional recognition of advance care planning documentation. Questions may therefore still arise as to the legal effect of previously expressed wishes, the authority of surrogate decision-makers and the relationship between patient autonomy, family input, best interests and emergency medical judgement. Similar concerns have also been raised in recent Malaysian clinical ethics scholarship, particularly in relation to the need for clearer guidance on capacity assessment, surrogate identification and the standards governing decisions made on behalf of incapacitated patients.[8]

[8] See, for instance, Tan (2025).

The revised Consent Guideline is significant because it introduces, in professional guidance form, the key elements that would ordinarily be expected in a legal framework on advance refusals of treatment, namely, clarity, applicability, capacity, voluntariness and documentation. It nevertheless remains a professional standard rather than a statutory rule. By contrast, the Mental Capacity Act 2005 in England and Wales gives clearer legal effect to advance decisions to refuse treatment, provided that they are valid and applicable to the circumstances that have arisen. The comparative value of that framework lies not in suggesting that it should be reproduced in Malaysia without modification but in illustrating the difference between professional recognition and legal enforceability.

Accordingly, the present Malaysian position may be characterised as one of significant normative and professional progress, but without full legal completion. What is now required is not merely a law on advance medical directives in isolation, but an integrated framework on advance care planning, advance decisions, surrogate decision-making and mental capacity, supported by professional guidance, clear institutional processes and adequate safeguards against misunderstanding or misuse. Such a framework would accord greater clarity to patients and families while at the same time providing medical practitioners with stronger legal assurance when acting in accordance with the patient's values, best interests and good medical practice.

5.3 Situating End-of-Life Care Within the Wider Context of Palliative Care

It is important to note that although this book focuses on end-of-life decisions, the delivery of care at this stage is in fact a component under the wider scope of palliative care. This position is now further reinforced by recent Malaysian policy materials. The National Palliative Care Policy and Strategic Plan 2019–2030 frames palliative care as a form of care that extends throughout the course of serious illness, and not only at the final stage of life.[9] More recent materials issued by the Ministry of Health similarly place emphasis on continuity of care, goals-of-care discussions and the transition between hospital, community and home-based services. This understanding is critical, as the decision-making process at the end of life would be less abrupt and more ethically coherent when it is situated within the earlier involvement of palliative care, rather than being left to be addressed only when the patient has entered the final phase of life.

The philosophy of palliative care in alleviating pain and suffering, as well as in providing support and assistance to patients and family members in the decision-making process, lies at the heart of end-of-life care. The notable difference remains that while palliative care may be delivered alongside curative or disease-modifying

[9] Medical Services Unit, Medical Development Division, Ministry of Health Malaysia (2019).

treatment throughout the illness trajectory, end-of-life care refers to palliative care that is delivered when the patient is in the final phase of life and definitive treatment is no longer beneficial. End-of-life decisions should therefore not be isolated so as to be dealt with primarily by the intensive care team at the latest stage of the disease trajectory. Rather, they require earlier and coordinated involvement by attending doctors, primary care practitioners, palliative care teams and, where appropriate, relevant subspecialists. This would allow symptom relief, communication, values discussions and future care planning to be undertaken in a more timely, coordinated and compassionate manner.

5.4 Future Directions for Regulatory Reform

The discussion in the preceding chapters lends credence to the view that reform in Malaysia should now proceed along two related lines. The first concerns the consolidation and refinement of professional and policy guidance, while the second relates to the gradual development of clearer legal standards to support such guidance. The recent materials issued by the Ministry of Health and the Malaysian Medical Council indicate that meaningful progress has already been made in the former respect. It is submitted, however, that such progress should now be consolidated in a coherent manner, so that the remaining areas of ambiguity may be addressed, and the normative principles reflected in current guidance may be supported by workable systems of implementation.

5.4.1 Consolidating Professional Guidance and National Standards into a Coherent End-of-Life Decision-Making Framework

The issuance of the ACP Guide, the Consent Guideline, the National Palliative Care Policy and Strategic Plan 2019–2030, the palliative care handbook materials and the recently issued National Standards for Palliative Care with Implementation Guide ("National Standards") collectively indicate that Malaysia has moved towards a more structured and patient-centred framework. These developments represent an important progression from the earlier position, where relevant guidance was largely dispersed across ethical codes, ICU protocols, palliative care handbooks and professional practice documents.

Nevertheless, it is submitted that the need for consolidation remains. The existing materials, while significant, do not yet constitute a single and coherent end-of-life decision-making pathway. The ACP Guide provides detailed guidance on advance care planning and future care preferences. The Consent Guideline addresses consent, mental capacity, surrogate involvement, advance medical directives and best interests. The National Standards, on the other hand, are directed more broadly towards strengthening and standardising palliative care services.[10] What remains necessary is to align these instruments in a manner that gives healthcare practitioners clearer guidance on the practical and ethico-legal steps to be taken when difficult end-of-life decisions arise.

Such a consolidated framework should therefore not duplicate the existing ACP Guide or National Standards. Rather, it should draw from them and set out, in one accessible pathway, the relevant principles and procedures on withholding and withdrawal of life-sustaining treatment, palliative sedation, goals-of-care discussions, advance care planning, assessment of mental capacity, surrogate involvement, family disagreement, cultural and religious considerations, documentation, escalation for ethics or legal advice and resource-sensitive decision-making. This would allow the present body of guidance to operate in a more coordinated manner while preserving sufficient flexibility for clinical judgement and local circumstances.

In the same vein, future Malaysian guidance, policy documents and legislative provisions should continue to avoid the use of the term "passive euthanasia" to describe the lawful and ethical withholding or withdrawal of non-beneficial treatment, unless what is being described is an omission carried out with the clear intent to cause death. This would be consistent with the direction taken in recent local guidance, which distinguishes euthanasia from treatment limitation and palliative measures by reference to intention. The continued avoidance of such terminology would serve an important clarificatory function, by reducing confusion among patients and families and reassuring doctors that the withholding or withdrawal of non-beneficial treatment, when carried out in accordance with good medical practice and the patient's best interests, is not to be misdescribed as euthanasia.

Recent local research on quality indicators for end-of-life cancer care also supports the need for such alignment. A consolidated framework would not only clarify professional obligations but also provide a more coherent basis for audit, service evaluation and quality improvement across institutions.[11]

5.4.2 Integrating Religious and Cultural Considerations into End-of-Life Guidance

The importance of religious and cultural values cannot be underestimated in the decision-making process at the end of life, due to its broad and significant impact on the delivery of holistic and compassionate care. It remains imperative that modules related to different religious perspectives and practices on end-of-life decisions are incorporated as part of the uniform guidelines, as well as healthcare training courses and programmes. The present Malaysian materials are more attentive than before to

[10] See Ministry of Health Malaysia (2025).

[11] See Wong et al. (2025).

person-centeredness and cultural sensitivity, but they still do not sufficiently set out how healthcare practitioners are to navigate religiously inflected preferences and concerns when confronting decisions about resuscitation, artificial nutrition and hydration, palliative sedation, place of death or the discontinuation of burdensome treatment.

The earlier recommendation therefore remains apposite: the relevant parts of the local palliative care materials touching on religion and culture should be expanded into proper manuals or modules specifically dealing with end-of-life issues from the different religious contexts in Malaysia. Input as to how each religion views end-of-life decisions should be included in order to guide healthcare practitioners in understanding and dealing with the needs and sensitivities of patients and families and to facilitate the shared decision-making process. In the Malaysian setting, such work would be best undertaken through consultation between the Ministry of Health, the Malaysian Medical Council, professional bodies and the respective religious authorities.

5.4.3 Providing Legal Safeguards for End-of-Life Decision-Making

The ethical guidelines in the UK and Australia remain instructive in that they set out the legal standards on end-of-life decisions as laid down in statutory provisions and judicial precedents. In Malaysia, as highlighted above, the legal standards on the same subject matter are still not manifested in the form of clear statutory provisions or case law. The legality of active euthanasia may be inferred from the Penal Code, but the legitimacy of withholding and withdrawing treatment, symptom relief that may foreseeably shorten life and the implementation of advance decisions remain insufficiently articulated in law.

For this reason, the need for clearer legal safeguards remains persuasive. One possible approach is the enactment of a carefully drafted protective provision within the existing criminal law framework. Such a provision need not amount to a comprehensive statute on end-of-life care at the outset. Rather, it may operate in a more limited manner by affirming that a doctor does not incur criminal liability where he or she withholds or withdraws non-beneficial treatment or administers palliative treatment for the relief of pain or distress, provided that the act is done in good faith, with reasonable care and skill and in accordance with proper professional standards. This would provide legal assurance to doctors while preserving the flexibility required in clinical decision-making.

Such an approach would also maintain an appropriate balance between law and professional judgement. The law need not prescribe every clinical step to be taken at the end of life. Its role should instead be to affirm the governing principles, protect patients from abuse and provide legal protection for doctors who act ethically and professionally. Properly framed, a statutory safeguard would complement, rather than replace, ethical codes and clinical guidelines. It would also encourage compliance, since legal protection would depend upon adherence to recognised standards of good medical practice.

This would also align better with present developments. Since professional guidance has now become more developed, especially in relation to consent, supported decision-making, surrogate involvement and advance decisions, the law may focus on affirming core safeguards while leaving detailed clinical processes to professional guidance and institutional protocols.

5.4.4 Regulating Advance Care Planning and Advance Medical Directives

In end-of-life care, ethical and legal dilemmas are exacerbated when discussions must involve family members who may be unprepared to shoulder the burden of decision-making or who may be in disagreement as to what the patient would have wanted. The ACP Guide has laid important groundwork by encouraging values-based discussions, the identification of surrogate decision-makers, documentation and review as part of the process of future care planning.[12]

It is submitted, however, that further regulation remains necessary. First, there should be clearer rules as to the status of the different forms of advance expression. The current professional position recognises written advance decisions and earlier expressed wishes, but Malaysia still lacks a statutory framework defining the validity, applicability, revocation and legal effect of such decisions. There is also a need to clarify the relationship between prior wishes, present wishes, surrogate input and the patient's best interests. Second, there should be a more precise legal framework on mental capacity and substitute decision-making, so that clinicians are not left to rely on professional guidance when faced with patients who no longer possess decision-making capacity but have left some indication of their wishes.

Comparative experience is instructive in this respect because it demonstrates that advance refusals of treatment and healthcare proxy decision-making are not necessarily regulated in the same way. In England and Wales, the Mental Capacity Act 2005 separates advance decisions to refuse treatment from lasting powers of attorney for health and welfare and gives each a defined legal effect. Australian legislation similarly illustrates how matters such as formalities, revocation, applicability, substitute decision-making and protection of doctors may be addressed through statute. These models should not be replicated in Malaysia without qualification, but they show the type of procedural safeguards that may be required if advance medical directives are to operate with legal certainty.

The ACP Guide also indicates the practical steps that should be further developed in the Malaysian context. It emphasises the importance of regular review,

[12] See Ministry of Health Malaysia (2024).

communication with loved ones, identification of a surrogate decision-maker, documentation in an accessible form and the gradual development of supporting documents such as statement-of-wishes forms, proxy contact details and preferences relating to life-sustaining treatment. The Consent Guideline similarly requires that treatment decisions for patients who lack mental capacity be made in their best interests and that efforts to identify a suitable surrogate decision-maker be properly documented. These developments should not be treated as substitutes for legal reform. Rather, they provide a sound basis upon which legislation and institutional systems may now be further developed.

The significance of the proposed Mental Capacity Bill should also be understood in this context. The current public position, as reflected in post-2024 policy discussions, suggests that a mental capacity bill remains under consideration. If enacted, such legislation could provide the much-needed legal structure for capacity assessment, supported decision-making, surrogate appointment, best-interests decision-making and the legal status of advance decisions. It is therefore submitted that future reform in Malaysia should ensure that advance care planning is integrated with the development of mental capacity legislation, rather than being treated as a separate or merely incidental matter.

5.4.5 Strengthening End-of-Life Care Strategies in Malaysia

A further matter that warrants fuller consideration concerns the strategies by which end-of-life care in Malaysia may be strengthened, so that financial limitations and resource constraints do not become decisive factors in determining whether a patient receives appropriate care. This issue is already implicit in the earlier discussion on medical futility, resource allocation and access to palliative care. Recent literature and policy developments, however, indicate that it should now be addressed more expressly as part of the broader reform agenda.

First, early and needs-based palliative care should be strengthened so that end-of-life decisions are not postponed until a crisis has already occurred. The recent Malaysian literature on accessibility, service availability and quality indicators lends support to this proposition. The 2024 mapping study on palliative care availability and accessibility in Malaysia shows that access remains uneven, particularly between urban and rural settings.[13] The earlier palliative care is introduced, the less likely it is that costly, burdensome and low-benefit interventions will become the default course of action merely because discussions were initiated too late. It is therefore important that healthcare institutions develop clearer mechanisms for identifying patients who may benefit from palliative care at an earlier stage and for initiating appropriate goals-of-care discussions before the patient enters the final phase of illness.

[13] See Segarmurthy et al. (2024).

Second, the delivery of palliative and end-of-life care should continue to move towards decentralisation, greater primary care involvement and stronger community-based support. As discussed earlier, Malaysian palliative care policy has increasingly recognised the need for integrated, domiciliary and community-based services, while recent local research continues to show disparities in geographical access to palliative care. This is particularly significant in Malaysia, since a patient's preferred place of care or death may not be realistically accommodated if palliative care services remain concentrated in specialist centres located mainly in urban areas. Community and home-based models of care are therefore not merely matters of convenience but form part of a fairer and more continuous system of care that is better able to respect the patient's values and preferences.

Third, resource allocation at the end of life should be guided by clear ethical principles and transparent service standards, rather than being left to be determined by financial pressures in individual cases. The issue is not simply that resources are limited, since scarcity is an unavoidable reality in any healthcare system. The more important question is how such limitations are to be managed in a manner that is ethically defensible. In this respect, the principle of distributive justice requires that scarcity should not operate indirectly through delayed referral, geographical exclusion, inadequate communication or the absence of alternatives to hospital-based care. Instead, healthcare institutions should develop clearer triggers for palliative care referral, pathways for goals-of-care discussions and internal review mechanisms in cases where intensive treatment is continued despite poor prognosis and minimal clinical benefit. This would make the ethical basis of such decisions more visible and reduce the risk that financial limitations become the unstated determinant of care.

Fourth, mechanisms for audit and quality improvement should also form part of end-of-life care strategies. As noted earlier, recent Malaysian research on quality indicators for end-of-life cancer care provides a useful basis for this purpose. By identifying indicators that are locally endorsed and sensitive to the Malaysian context, such work may assist healthcare institutions in assessing whether end-of-life care is delivered in a manner that is timely, coordinated and responsive to the needs of patients and families. This is particularly relevant in evaluating whether communication is adequate, whether palliative involvement occurs at an appropriate stage and whether disparities in access continue to affect the quality of care received. It is therefore submitted that the implementation of end-of-life care strategies should be accompanied by periodic institutional and national review based on agreed quality indicators.[14]

Fifth, there is also a need to reduce the use of low-benefit and burdensome interventions near the end of life. As discussed earlier, this should not be understood as rationing in disguise, but as part of the ethical requirement that treatment remains proportionate to the patient's condition, goals and best interests. Recent literature on the de-implementation of low-value end-of-life care and local Malaysian work on

[14] See Wong et al. (2025).

deprescribing for patients nearing the end of life demonstrate that the refinement of end-of-life care strategies is not confined to decisions concerning ventilators, resuscitation or intensive care. It also extends to everyday prescribing practices and treatment burdens, which may affect the patient's comfort, dignity and quality of care.[15]

Sixth, doctors and healthcare institutions should be supported in carrying out these responsibilities through training, communication frameworks and multidisciplinary assistance. As discussed earlier, the ethical burdens in end-of-life care are not borne by patients and family members alone. Recent Malaysian work on physicians' understanding of suffering at the end of life illustrates that doctors who repeatedly manage dying patients and distressed families may themselves experience emotional and professional strain. End-of-life care strategies should therefore include support for the clinicians who are expected to implement them, including training in communication, access to ethics consultation and team-based deliberation.[16]

Finally, the development of advance care planning in Malaysia should also be understood as part of this broader strategy to strengthen access, fairness and appropriate use of healthcare resources. Properly conducted advance care planning does not merely vindicate patient autonomy. It may also reduce decisional conflict, prevent clearly non-beneficial interventions, enable earlier support in the community and improve the alignment between available resources and the patient's values and goals. This, however, must not be framed as a cost-saving measure. The ethical legitimacy of advance care planning lies in person-centred care. Any saving of resources or improvement in efficiency should therefore be treated only as a secondary consequence of better, more proportionate and more humane decision-making.

5.5 Conclusion

The advancement of end-of-life care in Malaysia still requires the construction of a holistic regulatory framework on end-of-life decisions, in order to provide guidance and protection to doctors while ensuring that patient autonomy, dignity, welfare and best interests are properly respected. This central conclusion continues to hold true, although it must now be viewed against the more recent developments in Malaysian palliative and end-of-life care. What has changed is that the regulatory position is no longer as fragmented as before, with current guidance on advance care planning, consent, palliative care standards and professional decision-making providing a more structured basis for clinical practice.

Even so, the present framework has yet to fully address all aspects of end-of-life decision-making in Malaysia. There remain questions regarding the legal status of advance decisions and legal proxies, the precise legal standards applicable to

[15] See Chin et al. (2026).

[16] See Sinnathamby et al. (2026).

withholding and withdrawal of treatment, the uneven accessibility of palliative and end-of-life care services and the need for a coherent national pathway that integrates ethical, legal and clinical guidance. It is therefore submitted that the most constructive way forward is not to treat professional guidance and legislation as mutually exclusive alternatives. Rather, both are required: a more integrated and authoritative practice framework on the one hand and carefully framed legal reform on the other.

In practical terms, future reform should proceed by building upon the developments that are already taking place. This would require a closer integration between palliative care and end-of-life care, the continued avoidance of misleading terminology such as "passive euthanasia", the consolidation of existing guidance into a coherent framework and a deeper emphasis on communication, cultural competence and shared decision-making. It would also require clearer legal protection for doctors, the integration of advance care planning within future mental capacity reform and service strategies that promote equitable access to palliative and end-of-life care. These measures would help ensure that financial constraints do not become an unstated determinant of care at the end of life.

The immediate reform task is therefore not necessarily to codify every aspect of end-of-life care but to settle a limited number of recurrent legal questions: capacity, best interests, surrogate authority, advance refusals, documentation and the protection of doctors who act in good faith and in accordance with recognised professional standards. Clearer law and clearer professional guidance perform different functions and should therefore be developed in tandem rather than treated as substitutes for one another. In that sense, the present moment offers an important opportunity. The foundations are now more visible than before, and the remaining task is to build upon them coherently in a manner that is consistent with Malaysia's legal order, professional realities and plural social fabric.

References

Chin AAH, Lai PSM, McCarthy SA (2026) Deprescribing for patients nearing end of life: views, barriers and facilitators of palliative care patients, carers and nurses. Support Care Cancer 34:303. https://doi.org/10.1007/s00520-026-10522-3

Malaysian Medical Council (2025) Consent for treatment of patients by registered medical practitioners. https://mmc.gov.my/wp-content/uploads/2025/09/Consent-for-Treatment-of-Patients-by-Registered-Medical-Practitioners.pdf. Accessed 26 Apr 2026

Medical Services Unit, Medical Development Division, Ministry of Health Malaysia (2019) National palliative care policy and strategic plan 2019–2030. Ministry of Health Malaysia

Ministry of Health Malaysia (2024) Advance care planning: a guide for healthcare practitioners in Malaysia. Medical Development Division, Ministry of Health Malaysia

Ministry of Health Malaysia (2025) National standards for palliative care with implementation guide. Medical Development Division, Ministry of Health Malaysia

Segarmurthy MV, Lim RB-L, Yeat CL et al (2024) Mapping palliative care availability and accessibility: a first step to eradicating access deserts in the low- and middle-income settings. J Palliat Care 39(4):255–263. https://doi.org/10.1177/08258597231214485

Sinnathamby A, Ong YT, Lim SX et al (2026) Concepts of suffering at the end of life amongst emergency, palliative care and geriatric medicine physicians in Malaysia. Am J Hosp Palliat Med 43(1):85–93. https://doi.org/10.1177/10499091251317725

Tan MKM (2025) Determining mental capacity and identifying surrogates: the need for clearer guidance on medical decision-making in Malaysia. Asian Bioethics Review 17:117–128. https://doi.org/10.1007/s41649-024-00313-5

Wong WJ, Hwong WY, Teoh CCO et al (2025) Stakeholder consensus of quality indicators for end-of-life cancer care in Malaysia: a modified Delphi study. BMC Palliat Care 24:311. https://doi.org/10.1186/s12904-025-01947-4

MIX
Papier aus verantwortungsvollen Quellen
Paper from responsible sources
FSC® C105338

If you have any concerns about our products,
you can contact us on
ProductSafety@springernature.com

In case Publisher is established outside the EU,
the EU authorized representative is:
Springer Nature Customer Service Center GmbH
Europaplatz 3, 69115 Heidelberg, Germany

Printed by Libri Plureos GmbH
in Hamburg, Germany